# Nostalgic Memories
## of
# LIVERPOOL

*The publishers would like to thank the following companies for their*

*support in the production of this book*

## Main sponsor
## Halewood International Ltd

Alfred Price & Sons

Bibby Line Group

Eli Lilly

Griffiths & Armour

Henry Bath & Son

Herbert of Liverpool

Jaguar Land Rover

John Mason International

Knowsley Safari Park

LBK Packaging

Liverpool Hope University

Merchant Taylors' Schools

Merseyside Fire and Rescue Services

The Millgrain Group

Nugent Care

Nutricia

Silverbeck Rymer Solicitors

Wrenco Construction

First published in Great Britain by True North Books Limited
England HX3 6SN
01422 244555
**www.truenorthbooks.com**

ISBN 978 - 1906649685

Text, design and origination by True North Books
Printed and bound by The Amadeus Press

# Nostalgic Memories
## of
# LIVERPOOL

# CONTENTS

# INTRODUCTION

Welcome to the treat that lies in store within the following pages. 'Nostalgic Memories of Liverpool' is the latest in a series of True North publications about our wonderful city. Such has been the popularity of our previous books on the Liverpool area, that we have been encouraged to produce a new publication. Turning over leaf after leaf will bring you to a treasure trove from the last century. With stunning images, backed up by interesting and thought provoking text, this book opens the door to the days when our parents and grandparents were helping make the world and shape the city that we know today. Our books allow readers to walk on cobbled streets, browse in well known local shops of the period and revisit special events and occasions, without leaving the comfort of their favourite armchair. Readers will be taken back to their own youth and beyond in a delightful journey that will jog memories and bring back recollections of things that we had all but forgotten. They may highlight an event described to us by a close relative or they could feature historical landmarks such as bridges and buildings. Once more there will be tripe on sale at Graham's market stall, furs to buy at Swears and Wells on Church Street and a fine Wolseley to drive out of Prout's car showroom in Everton.

The title of this new book, 'Nostalgic Memories of Liverpool', tells you all you need to know about what is captured within its pages. We feel this publication is largely a celebration of what made our birthplace a great place to be and somewhere we are proud to mention when we are away from home.

Despite being England's third largest city, it was, for many centuries, something of a backwater. Founded as a borough in 1207 during the reign of King John, it still only boasted a population of about 500 in Tudor times. It was with the silting up of the Dee estuary that attention turned to Merseyside as a viable alternative. In William III's reign, Liverpool began to advance in size, population and commerce. An act was passed in 1699 by which Liverpool became a parish.

The first commercial wet dock was built in Liverpool in the early 18th century and trade flourished in this quickly developing port. Previously ships were simply tied up by the shore but as the port grew busier this was no longer adequate. Liverpool grew to be the third largest port in the country behind London and Bristol. Sadly and shamefully, much of the business and prosperity was based on the highly profitable slave trade. The port continued to grow and more honest goods were shipped in and out, helping Liverpool to develop into a world leader during the 19th century. The population grew rapidly and we were awarded city status in 1880. By then, the nature of the citizens as a cosmopolitan mix of different ethnic backgrounds was well established. With our own distinctive dialect and accent as well, we Liverpuddlians are proud of our individuality as Britons second and Scousers first and foremost.

The photographs within this book link events, places and people from the last century, with particular emphasis on the first two thirds of that era. They will help the reader recall times when the pace of life was that little bit slower and neighbours actually knew one another and took the time to chat. You will come across pictures of children making up games to play in the street without parents fussing over them and being over-protective. Shopkeepers sold spuds by the pound and boiled ham by the quarter. We handed over our bobs and tanners and bought our beer in pints poured from a jug or pulled by hand through a pump.

Liverpool has always been a vibrant city, buzzing with energy, but different episodes in its life can be seen here. It is fun to compare past with present and argue about which aspects have changed for the better or otherwise. So put a 78 on the gramophone or turn on the wireless and tune in to 'Housewives' Choice' on the Light Programme. Reminisce about youthful days dancing at the Grafton Ballroom or courting in the cinemas of old and be entertained once again…Happy memories!

DEUS NOBIS HAEC OTIA FECIT

| | |
|---|---|
| TEXT | ANDREW MITCHELL, STEVE AINSWORTH, TONY LAX |
| PHOTOGRAPH RESEARCH | TONY LAX |
| DESIGNER | SEAMUS MOLLOY |
| BUSINESS DEVELOPMENT MANAGER | PETER PREST |

# STREET SCENES

**Above and top right:** The tramlines headed straight along Castle Street to the junction with Dale Street to the right and Water Street to the left. These latter two are among the city's seven original streets, with Dale Street being so named because it led to a dale through which a stream flowed from Moss Lake. The Town Hall is instantly recognisable at the top of Castle Street and little else has changed in the years that have passed in the interim. The curved arch entrance on the left is still home to a bank, currently the NatWest, while the arcade entrance to Queen Avenue opposite is clearly seen. The Town Hall that John Wood the Elder designed in the late 18th century originally had a square structure instead of a dome. This was demolished in 1786 and the new round one added after the fire of 1795 that had badly damaged the building. In the companion photograph, the former Martins Bank can be seen, next to the Town Hall. The building, designed by Herbert Rowse, was erected in 1932 and was home to the former Bank of Liverpool and Martins Ltd that could trace its financial roots to the 16th century. The name was shortened in 1928. During the last war much of the nation's gold was stored in the vaults here. The bank

was taken over by Barclays in 1969, but that company ceased to do business from here during the first decade of this century.

## Did you know?

*The last act of the American Civil War was the surrender of the Confederate warship Shenandoah. The ship captained by Lieutenant Waddell arrived in Liverpool on 6 November, 1865.*

**Right:** With Liverpool Central Station to the right, that side of Ranelagh Street, viewed from Hanover Street, has had some alterations over the years. The once mighty Lewis's department store, further along at No 40, resisted change over the intervening decades. Founded by David Lewis in 1856, this incarnation was built to replace the one damaged by bombs during the last war. By 1951, a new elegant store opened. Built of Portland stone, it was completed with marble clad hallways and fluted columns. The building had an internal area of over 500,000 square feet and boasted four passenger lifts complete with lift attendants. In 1953, restaurants were opened on the fifth floor. The Lewis empire spread across the country, but began to fall on hard times and store after store closed towards the end of the last century. Liverpool's flagship store shut its doors in June 2010. The other side of Ranelagh Street looks much the same as it did in the early 1950s, though the businesses now include Millets instead of Charles and Co and an amusement arcade next to Henrys. This street took its name from the 17th century Earl of Ranelagh. He gave his name to pleasure gardens in Chelsea that in turn gave their name to tea gardens established where the Adelphi Hotel was built on Ranelagh Place in 1914 .The handsome cupola in the distance belongs to The Vines, opened in 1867 and refurbished in this Edwardian baroque style in 1907. It is known to locals as 'the big house'.

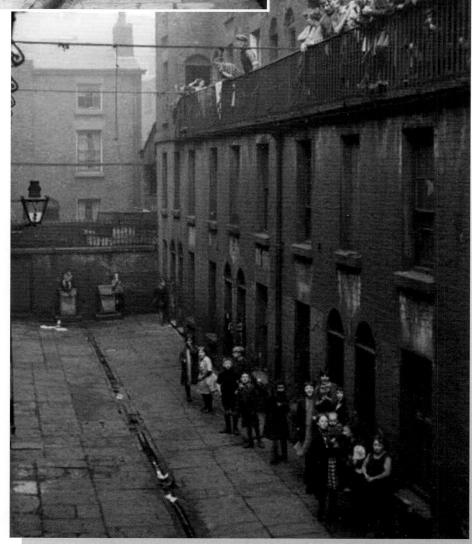

**Above and right:** The people on the balcony and the children below on the flagstones of Dickson Terrace, off Soho Street in the L3 district, seemed happy enough. Perhaps they knew no better. Their living conditions were poor, cramped and overcrowded with little in the way of modern amenities. These slums of the early 1930s were hardly the homes fit for heroes that Prime Minister Lloyd George had promised at the end of the First World War. Liverpool built a number of council houses during this time, but it was nowhere near enough. The faces on the trio of residents by No 3 Court, Clayton Street, photographed about the same time, suggest a life of struggle and woe. The caged bird might have been singing, but these people had nothing to warble or even smile about. It was a tough life and eviction was a distinct possibility. Clayton Street used to back onto the Walker Art Gallery and was demolished just before the last war. It was named for the family of William Clayton, a local 18th century MP. His daughter, Sarah, also helped design the layout of Clayton Square.

speed grass tracks separated the trams from the rest of the traffic.

**Below:** Dale Street is one of the city's main arterial thoroughfares, running all the way from the Town Hall to the Central Library. The first few years of the post-war period in mid-20th century Britain was a time of austerity and continued rationing. We could not even sleep peacefully in our beds as the threat of communism and warmongers such as Joseph Stalin posed a threat to world order. The coal mines, railways, some road transport and power supplies were all brought under government control, to be followed shortly afterwards by the iron and steel industries. Even so, those baby boomer years did bring us secondary education for all and the National Health Service came into being. For these latter blessings, Liverpuddlians hurrying along Dale Street were heartily thankful.

**Above:** You wait for ages and then half a dozen appear at the same time. The line of trams on Water Street in about 1930 would seem to support this statement. Liverpool trams can trace their history back to 1869 when 16 horse drawn vehicles were ushered into service. After electrification of the tracks at the turn into the 20th century, a clear connection can be made between this new mode of transport and dwelling patterns. The very shape of the growth and development of our city mirrored the extending fingers of the tram tracks. They showed where traders, sailors, financiers and merchants lived and the routes they took to their places of work. During the inter-war years, the tram system was invaluable to the local economy, offering a cheap and reliable means of public transport. Over 300 new cars were built at Edge Lane in the 1930s. In the suburbs, high

## Did you know?

*The first travelling Post Office (a horse box fitted out as a sorting office) ran between Liverpool and Birmingham on 6 January, 1838.*

# Lord Street

This collection shows Lord Street as it changed from before the First World War to the face it presented to the city in the period immediately following the Second World War. A look along the street towards Whitechapel and Church Street in 1922 completes the set. This highway was once known as Molyneux Lane or Lord Molyneux Street. This was the family name of the Earls of Sefton. William Molyneux, the second Earl, was an enthusiastic gambler and sportsman. He helped establish Aintree as a racecourse and also founded the Waterloo Cup, a prize event in coursing. The family had a house on the north side of what became Lord Street. After that dwelling was demolished, Commerce Court was built on the site and the family crest, carved in stone, was retained there. This was all lost during action in World War II. The earliest photograph displays an uneasy alliance between the horse and electricity as a means of power. It was not to last and such private cabs and taxis would be a rarity by the time of the Great War. As well as providing a public service, trams were used to advertise goods, products and local businesses. The one leading the way in 1922 was recommending the virtues of MacSymons Stores. An even more memorable store can be seen in the most modern of this set of images. Bunneys, on the corner with Whitechapel and Church Street, called itself 'The Gift House' and was where you could get something for almost anyone. Its distinctive face was lost when it was demolished in the late 1950s.

# Church Street

C hurch Street which takes its name from St Peters, a church consecraited in 1704 and demolished in 1923, is now part of the retail area of the city centre designated as a pedestrian zone. Traffic is banned and shoppers can walk around the paved areas in comparative safety. Back in 1925, the motorcar was still something of an occasional sight, so the open topped model would have been a novelty and turned a few heads. Out of way of the confines of the city, the driver could let his hair down and whiz along the country lanes like Mr Toad in his wildest moments. The interwar equivalent of a Hooray Henry loved to don a pair of driving gloves and even a version of a pair of flying goggles as he roared off, anxious to impress one of the flapper generation of more liberated 'gals'. In the photograph (top left) from 1940s', we can see the building used by Russell's at 18 Church Street. This was a family firm of clock and watch makers founded in early Victorian times. Originally on Slater Street, the business moved here in 1877.

# Parker Street

These scenes show the unchanging face of Parker Street, pictured just after the end of each of the world wars. Other than the vehicles we can observe and the clothing fashion we can make out, all else might have been in some form of time warp. On closer examination, perhaps we can also determine a different balance between the types of vehicles to be spotted. There are only a couple of cars in the older photograph and considerably more in the later one. The names on some of the shop facades changed, but little has otherwise altered. Reece's is one famous name, clearly visible on the top left of the view from the early 1920s, that might stir a few memories. This family business had a number of cafés, restaurants and confectionery interests across Merseyside. Samuel Reece, a dairyman, founded the business in the 19th century. The modern Parker Street has lost its trams, buses and cars long ago as it became part of the shopper-only reserve that is now the face of modern retail areas in the city heartland.

# Lime Street

This group of pictures show Lime Street during the interwar years, seen from different perspectives. The handsome clock to the right of the road leading down to St George's Hall is still ticking away happily today above the entrance to The Vines, the pub opened by Albert Vines nearly 150 years ago. It was taken over by Walker's Brewery in the early 1900s and still advertises its Warrington Ales today. The Fifty Shilling Tailor occupied the site on the opposite corner, selling fixed price suits at an affordable price. In more modern times, the Kumar Brothers Store was opened here. In the other scenes, St George's Place provides the focus. One photograph shows St George's Hall with the impressive and imposing former Great North Western Hotel that provided accommodation for travellers using Lime Street Station. Built in 1867 by Alfred Waterhouse, the architect who also designed London's Natural History Museum and Manchester Town Hall, the hotel has, in more recent times, been turned into student flats. A pub occupies part of the ground floor, a fact often celebrated by the young residents above. Finally, looking across from the Washington Hotel, the collection of vehicles might just have been lifted from the old television series 'The Untouchables' when actor Robert Stack as Eliot Ness hunted down gangsters who machine gunned all and sundry standing on the running boards of cars such as these.

# William Brown Street

**W**illiam Brown Street was originally known as Shaw's Brow and was one of the principal coaching roads east from the city. It was renamed in honour of the merchant, banker and philanthropist who was born in Ireland in 1784. He emigrated to America in 1800, but came to Liverpool in 1809 to establish a branch of the family investment bank. He also diversified, trading in cotton and linen in addition to his financial interests. He became the Member of Parliament for South Lancashire in 1846. Brown used his wealth to help fund the town's museum and public library in 1860. He was ennobled by being created the 1st Baronet of Richmond Hill and died in Liverpool in 1864. The street that bears his name is seen in early Edwardian times and, again, nearly 50 years later in 1951, towards the end of the reign of King George VI. By then, the place was much cleaner. The muck on the roads, much of it from horse droppings, was no longer one of the accepted norms on the surfaces of thoroughfares. Today the William Brown Street Conservation Area forms the principal cultural quarter, where there is a high concentration of the city's major public buildings.

**Above:** A familiar sight to motorists in the mid 1950s, to see a policeman directing traffic from his black and white striped box. This was the time when we had the reassurance that a local "bobby" was stationed in most towns and villages. They were happy to leave the safety of their Panda cars and risk life and limb on point duty at busy traffic junctions. Shoppers in this busy scene from 1955 rush along Church Street in what was Liverpool's main shopping area, lying between Bold Street to the East and Lord Street to the West. Over the years it has been the host to many of the city's main High Street stores, including such names as, Bon Marche, George Henry Lee, Bunney's, Woolworths and M&S, to name but a few. No real need for a policeman in the picture, top right, which comes from the same area of Church Street around 1975, just after pedestrianisation. Road markings are still visible and people are still crossing the road in an orderly fashion, probably because of habit.

**Below, facing page:** St George's Place by night in 1960-61 has a different face today. The scene is quite dramatic in its liveliness and in some ways it is quite reminiscent of London's Piccadilly Circus. The distinctive Guinness Clock provided an easy reference point outside the Imperial Hotel, for people arranging to meet up for a night out. Perhaps they would move further along Lime Street and enjoy time at the Forum Cinema, one of the city's best appointed picture houses that opened in 1931. With its 100-foot bronze canopy, white marble stairway and comfortable café, it was a popular spot

daring choice. The creation of St John's Shopping Centre at the end of the 1960s changed the face of St George's Place completely as much of what we can see here was swept away.

**Below:** This is a view from around 1970 of the original and aesthetically better looking Clayton Square. Clayton Square was named after William Clayton, who became Mayor of Liverpool in 1689 and subsequently, between 1698 and 1714, represented the borough in parliament. The square was created in his memory in the mid-1700s and originally consisted of exclusive housing. The poster outside The Jacey cinema is advertising Black Orpheus, a 1959 film about the Rio Carnival, but this is much later and shows the end of an

until 1998 when it showed its last reel. Next to the Guinness sign, that advertising Martell shone brightly on the Washington Hotel, a place where the Italian revolutionary Garibaldi is said to have once stayed. To its right, the Empress Chinese restaurant was a favoured eatery and one of our first ventures into the world of intercontinental cuisine. We think nothing today of tickling our taste buds with exotic meals from the Far East, but 50 years ago a plate of chicken chow mein and a couple of prawn crackers was a most

era for Brown's department store. The old Jacey Cinema was probably best known for its screening of adult films, with the occasional continental art film, before it closed in 1972. The building was subsequently transformed into a church, known as the Shrine of the Blessed Sacrament. The once familiar telephone boxes and taxi rank are also in evidence. In decades gone by, this was a site for the Christmas Tree and Salvation Army brass band, and many readers will remember with fondness St John's Market, which closed in 1964.

# ENTERTAINMENT LEISURE & PASTIMES

**Above and top right:** In Edwardian days, it was fashionable to take the air and promenade through Princes Park. Society ladies could show off their finery and courting couples were able to chat discreetly, though a chaperone of one sort or another often lingered in the background. Women still favoured long, near floor length dresses. They would be very feminine in appearance, with a curvaceous look. This was achieved at something of a cost as tightly laced corsets might have enhanced the female shape but they also restricted blood and air flow. Swooning was quite a common occurrence. The S-curve corset was popular in the early 1900s. Straight at the front, it had a pronounced curve at the back that forced the upper body forward and the rear end out. Princes Park was originally a private development. It was designed by a well known pair off architects, James Pennethorpe and Joseph Paxton. The former helped shape London's Battersea Park and the latter is best remembered for his work on the Crystal Palace. Princes Park opened in 1942, with its serpentine lake, wide, sweeping drive and a style that provided a blueprint for later Victorian parks and landscaped areas. The Sunburst Gates are still with us, but the Doric Lodge was blasted to smithereens in a German bomber raid during the Second World War.

**Right:** For many, New Brighton was as far afield as they could get when it came to going on holiday. Even though it is just across the river at the northern end of the Wirral peninsula, somehow the sand and sea breeze seemed that bit different from what we experienced on the other side of the Mersey. In 1889 it was a real adventure for these women who let their daughters lift their skirts and paddle in the Irish Sea. A little further out, the bathing hut provided a modesty screen for those who were daring enough to enter the briny and swim a short distance. The woman holding the parasol to protect her from the rays of the sun must have been roasting in her thick skirt and, presumably, heavy undergarments. At least she had managed to remove her jacket in an attempt to keep cool. New Brighton area was a popular Victorian resort for people from all over Lancashire, Cheshire and North Wales. The railways brought visitors here in large numbers and many of the large private houses in the vicinity were turned into hotels and guest houses. A pier was opened in the 1860s and a promenade from here to Seacombe created in the 1890s. Seafront entertainment was developed

to include funfair attractions, a circus, a ballroom and a lofty tower to rival and even outdo the one at Blackpool. Unfortunately, lack of maintenance during the 1914-18 War caused the closure of the tower in 1919. Even so, the resort continued to flourish until the middle of the last century when it fell out of favour with the general public.

## *Did you know?*

*The world's first crossword puzzle (word cross) was designed by a Liverpudlian Arthur Wynne and appeared in New York World*

**Above:** Several of the men relaxing outside the Customs House in 1890 were enjoying a pipeful of tobacco. The use of an old clay pipe and a well burned thumb to tamp down the hot embers were part and parcel of a dockworker's essential equipment. Smoking calmed the fevered brow and a pipe firmly clenched between the teeth was just one part of the working man's uniform. This group may well have had another reason than relaxation for a presence on these steps. The development of trade unionism was still in its infancy and shipyard owners and waterfront bosses were having their dictatorial authority challenged as ordinary men joined the struggle for better conditions and improved pay. In 1889, a strike by stevedores and dock labourers in the Port of London came to provide the catalyst and symbol for others with similar grievances to follow suit. The following year, Liverpool dockers became involved in a similarly large and protracted struggle. It had a deep and lasting effect on industrial relations on the Mersey waterfront. The fledgling National Union of Dock Labourers moved its headquarters to Liverpool in the early 1890s.

> ## Did you know?
> *The first cycling club to appear in Britain was in 1867 when the Liverpool Velocipede Club was formed.*

**Below:** These members of the Liverpool Century Road Club cut quite incongruous figures as they posed in Sefton Park. With plus twos instead of lycra shorts and with bicycle clips

keeping trouser turn-ups from snagging on the chain, this apparently exclusively male gathering prepared to face the open road. The rather distinctive headgear would not have passed muster for an early version of a safety helmet, safe to say. The club is still flourishing today and, with the United Kingdom's excellent showing at recent Olympics, the sport is enjoying a resurgence as budding Chris Hoys and Vicky Pendletons take to the saddle. The club was formed in 1916 and got its name form the expectation that members had to commit to being able to cycle at least 100 miles in a day. That is no longer a requirement, but new applicants are encouraged to cycle as much as possible.

**Above right and below:** Hell might not freeze over, but the lake in Sefton Park has. During one particularly harsh winter in the 1890s, locals took advantage of the conditions to get their ice skates out of mothballs and indulge in a bit of fun. Of course, you had to be a member of the middle classes to afford such luxuries. The parents of street urchins could not even afford shoes for them, never mind the sort of sporting kit to which they could never even aspire. Toboggans, tin trays and even bits of old carpet were used as vehicles on which to hurtle down the slopes, scattering all and sundry before them. In the later photograph, taken in 1936, the lake was being used for its intended purpose. The boathouse in the background has been replaced by a café, but much of the rest of this view is immediately familiar. Sefton Park is part of the historical Toxteth Royal Deer Park that eventually passed into the hands of the Earl of Sefton. In 1867, the Council bought 375 acres of land from the Earl. It opened as a park for 'the health and enjoyment of the townspeople' at a ceremony on 20 May, 1872, at which Prince Arthur, Duke of Connaught, officiated.

> ···· *Did you know?* ····
>
> *Goal nets were the invention of John Alexander Brodie, Liverpool's city engineer, who took out a patent for his invention in 1889.*

**Right:** The Marine Gardens, at Waterloo, near Crosby, provide a delightful series of landscaped areas along the seafront of Liverpool Bay. Within their confines, with the scent of salt in your nostrils and the shrubs and plants all around, the noise and bustle of the city seems a long way off. These children were far removed from both the urban environment and life as we know it today. The little boys had knees; not something you come across regularly in modern society where young lads are fully trousered from an early age. Girls, too, had legs. They often ended in what mum called 'sensible shoes' above which short socks were displayed. We wore our school uniforms with pride and these were symbols of our belonging to a larger society, one which we were thrilled to serve. We wore our caps or berets with distinction, though they would be stuffed into pockets as we got to our teenage years.

## *Did you know?*

*Liverpool St. Helens Football Club traces its origins to 1857 when Liverpool Football Club was formed and lays claim to be the oldest, continuously open rugby club in the World.*

*Liverpool footballer Jack Balmer holds the Football League record as the first player to score three consecutive hat-tricks. Born in West Derby, he achieved the record in November 1946.*

**Bottom left:** The Palm House was given to Liverpool as a gift from Henry Yates Thompson, the grand nephew of the founder of Princes Park. It was designed by the Edinburgh firm, Mackenzie and Moncur and was completed in 1896. The 'Great Conservatory' took the place of the band pavilion and with its exotic plants and stunning statues; it soon became the centre piece of Sefton Park. At the outset of war in 1939, The Palm House was camouflaged in case the glass would reflect the moonlight and act as a

**Below:** When this photograph of the Odeon, London Road, was taken, the cinema was just 20 years old. The cinema was built in 1930s on the site of a boxing stadium that had closed in 1931 and opened as the Paramount in 1934. At the opening show there was a personal appearance by one of Paramount's biggest British movie stars, Ida Lupino. The Art Deco style cinema was designed for a single screen with stalls and a circle, a large cafe and a resident organist. In 1942, Paramount

guide for enemy planes. During the Blitz in May 1941, a bomb fell shattering almost all the glass but luckily the structure of the building stood firm. When £2.5 million was awarded by the Heritage Lottery Fund, the complete restoration was made possible. Work commenced in spring 2000 and on 6 September, 2001, the Palm House was officially re-opened.

sold the cinema to the Odeon Deutsch group and it was renamed the Odeon. In 1954, the year of the photograph, it became the first Merseyside cinema to be equipped for CinemaScope films. Following a record run of The Sound of Music, the cinema converted to twin screens. The Odeon enjoyed world fame when, in July, 1964, it was used for the première of the Beatles' film A Hard Day's Night. The arrival of the Fab Four for the screening, at the height of Bealtemania, brought the city to a standstill. Additional screens were added over a 25-year period, but falling demand for huge auditoriums and rival out-of-town multiplexes led to the Odeon gradually becoming a multi-screen cinema; by 1999 it had 10 screens. This was to mark the end of development and the opening of Odeon's new cinema in Liverpool One was the end of the road for a cinema that had provided great entertainment for over 60 years.

---

## *Did you know?*

*Liverpool holds the Guinness Book of Records for being the capital of pop music – more Liverpool artists have had a number one hit than any other town or city in the world.*

*In 1953 Liverpool's Lita Roza was the first British female singer to top the UK singles charts with (how Much is) 'That Doggy in the Window', a cover version of Patti Page's original.*

Running down from St George's church, between Northumberland Terrace and Netherfield Road North, this street even had a handrail to help people puff their way up from the bottom. It is pictured, in all probability, in the early 1950s as there are no TV aerials in sight. But, children did not notice the less than perfect living conditions back then. They had more important things upon which to concentrate. If there was a game of soccer, usually played with coats as goalposts, then they had to decide whether to play like Roy Vernon or Jimmy Gabriel. Cricketers aped Brian Statham's fast bowling or Geoff Pullar's dour batting. Simple games were also very popular, especially ones that did not need fancy or expensive equipment. Children were happy to play hopscotch on a grid chalked on the pavement or with marbles that they kept in special bags. There were spinning tops and cries of 'What time is it Mr Wolf?' and kiddies racing around chasing and catching one another in British Bulldog or tag. They skipped over ropes and threw tennis balls against a wall, chanting rhymes about Gospel writers or tinkers and tailors. A healthy imagination was being used in the other photograph.

**Above:** Paperweight boxing championships - 11-month-old Stephen Williams became the paperweight champion of Panton Road, West Derby, Liverpool, when he defeated his greatest rival and next door neighbour Martin Langshaw (also 11 months old) in a straight fight over one round. Martin very obviously did not agree with the verdict and declared it a foul in no uncertain terms. Stephen the new champ on the other hand thought the whole thing a howling success.

### Did you know?

*In May 1958, Everton FC were the first English football club to install undersoil pitch heating.*

*It was Independence Day 1944 when world heavyweight boxing champion, Joe Louis became one of the esteemed names to have joined Liverpool Football Club.*

**Right and facing page:** The row of terraced houses running down Everton's Havelock Street is part of our history that included sub-standard properties that would eventually be subject to a slum clearance programme.

Boys as well as girls could dress up and imagine that their bikes and trikes were tanks, horses or chariots. The streets were their playground, as good as any council owned one with its pre-ordained swings and roundabouts.

### Did you know?

*Alder Hey Children's Hospital was founded in 1914 and is one of the largest hospitals in Europe, providing care for approximately 200,000 children and young people each year.*

"**A**m I bothered?!!..." Not even the construction of a massive new bridge is going to get in the way of these children enjoying a game of skipping. This scene from 1961 shows the youngsters oblivious to the mechanical magic taking shape behind them. The construction of the Silver Jubilee Bridge started on in 1956 and was opened on 21 July, 1961, by H.R.H. Princess Alexandra of Kent. The bridge crosses the River Mersey and the Manchester Ship Canal at Runcorn Gap between Runcorn and Widnes.

**Right:** This could have been just a trio of ordinary teenagers, posing for the camera in early 1960. At the time, they were friends who had been playing guitars as part of a skiffle group, the Quarrymen, that had been formed by John Lennon (centre). Being the oldest, he naturally assumed a leadership role, though this would be challenged in later years. George Harrison (left) was over two years younger and Paul McCartney (right), outside whose house the boys stood, came in between in terms of age. At this time such singers as Michael Holliday and Anthony Newley were topping the charts, but these lads were about to embark on a journey that would change all their lives and that of the modern music scene as well. Just over six months after this image was recorded, the boys would have metamorphosed through Long John and the Beetles and the Silver Beatles into the Beatles. They added Stuart Sutcliffe and Pete Best to their number and set off for Hamburg where they would cut their musical teeth and hone their professional act. Harrison was still only 17 and had to lie to the authorities in Germany about his age.

------- **Did you know?** -------

*The Beatles are the only musicians to achieve five Diamond albums, signifying U.S. sales of 10 million copies or more.*

However, the first visit was cut short after several mishaps, but the group returned and enjoyed several successful residencies at Hamburg clubs. Word about them spread and, when performing in their home city at the Cavern Club, they were signed up by manager Brian Epstein in early 1962. By then, Sutcliffe had left the group and Best had just a few months to go before being replaced. Richard Starkey, better know by his stage name of Ringo Starr, joined the band as drummer in August, 1962.

**Right:** Many readers will remember the day that alternative live music was born at No 10 Mathew Street in Liverpool. Alan Sytner opened the Cavern Club having been inspired by Paris's Jazz district where there were a number of clubs in cellars. He eventually found a perfect cellar for his club - which had been used as an air raid shelter during the war - and opened it on 16 January 1957. The opening act at the club was band called 'The Merseysippi Jazz Band', still going strong, and quite possibly Britain's longest surviving jazz ensemble. It is reported they played to a bulging 600 people, with double that amount locked out in the cold. The Cavern was an instant success. Within 3 years membership totalled an unparalleled 20,000 people, bands came to play there from all over the world. The Beatles made their first lunchtime appearance at the club on Tuesday 9 February 1961. They had returned to Liverpool from Hamburg. During the following 2 years, the Beatles made 292 appearances at the club, with their last occurring on 3 August, 1963, a month after the band recorded "She Loves You". Future star Cilla Black worked as the hat-check girl at The Cavern in her pre-fame days.

The original club closed in March 1973, and was filled in during construction work on the Merseyrail underground rail loop.

**Left and below:** The Punch and Judy man has been coming to Liverpool for over 150 years. In 1860, Richard Codman, a showman and puppeteer, was allowed to set up a show on the square known as The Quadrant, in between Lime Street Station and the market. Styling himself as 'Professor', a title adopted by many in his profession, Codman became a regular visitor with his show that was often seen in other towns and at various fairs and shows across the northwest. He continued in the business until his death in 1907, after which time his son, Richard Jnr, continued the tradition. The Liverpool-based Sandon Studios Society arranged in 1922 for a beautifully carved Punch and Judy booth to be created and this provided a delightful stage for performances of the irascible old puppet battering his wife and indulging in acts of mayhem involving a baby, a policeman, a crocodile, a hangman and the devil. After The Quadrant site was lost, the booth was temporarily housed in St. George's Hall and occasionally appeared in Williamson Square where it always attracted an appreciative audience. The latest Professor Codman is still producing strings of sausages today.

*Did you know?*

*At 67metres (220ft) above floor level, the bells of Liverpool Cathedral are the highest and heaviest ringing peal in the world.*

# BUILDINGS & MONUMENTS

**Left:** The Albert Dock is a complex of dock buildings and warehouses located to the south of the Pier Head. Designed by Jesse Hartley and Philip Hardwick and opened in 1846, the Albert Dock warehouses were the first in the world to be entirely fireproof, due to their construction from only iron, brick and stone, with no structural wood. The dock was home to many advances in docking technology including being the first to have hydraulic cranes. During World War II the buildings suffered significant damage and general docking decline in the city after the end of the war saw them fall rapidly into disrepair. In the 1980s the area underwent massive regeneration after the creation of the Merseyside Development Corporation and the complex was reopened to the public in 1984, as part of the tall ships festival. Today they form a focal point for tourism in the city, being home to the Tate Liverpool, Merseyside Maritime Museum and The Beatles Story. They also constitute the largest single collection of Grade I listed buildings anywhere in the UK.

## Did you know?

The Albert Dock opened by Prince Albert in 1846, now has the country's largest group of Grade 1 listed buildings.

**Top:** The Custom House was built between 1828 and 1839 by city architect John Foster on the site of the original Old Dock. It housed a post office, a telegraph office and offices for the Mersey Docks and Harbour Board. During the May Blitz of 1941, the building was heavily damaged by German fire bombs which gutted the interior and destroyed the dome. The loss of the Custom House was almost certainly Liverpool's greatest architectural casualty of the Second World War. The decision to demolish the shell of the building was met with widespread disapproval. There is controversy to this day about the extent of damage to the building and whether or not reconstruction would have been practical. The Liverpool Hilton Hotel now stands on the site of this former landmark.

**Above:** Originally opened in 1809, the Exchange Buildings occupy the site of two earlier Exchanges. Initially the space was used by merchants who gathered in the arches beneath the Town Hall, however preferring to transact business in the open air, they soon came to use the space which we now refer to as the Exchange Flags. The Exchange now consists of two distinctly varying groups of buildings. In the north-east corner of the Flags is the remaining part of the old Exchange, with attractive arcades opening on to the flags. On the west side of the Flags is the massive new building known as Derby House. The Nelson Monument, unveiled in 1813, was designed by Matthew Cotes Wyatt and sculpted by Richard Westmacott. The monument to Admiral Horatio Nelson was Liverpool's first piece of free-standing outdoor sculpture. Funded by public subscription, its real purpose was to celebrate the growing prestige of Liverpool, and its location at the Exchange served to remind the city's merchants of the protection afforded to their commercial interests by Nelson's naval achievements.

**Right:** The railways revolutionised British life in the Victorian era. They opened up speedier and more far ranging commercial links across the nation than ever had been possible using canals or horse drawn wagons. They also changed family life forever. Places that were a day's travel away became reachable in a couple of hours. More importantly, the age of steam provided mobility for people to go further afield to find work and make a new life for themselves. Families that had been a fixture in a town or village for centuries suddenly found that their relatives had moved away. Once it had been the norm never to venture more than a few miles from where you were born, but, when the locomotives came to call, there was no stopping the exodus from more rural areas. With its pioneering place in railway history established when the Rocket made its famous run at Rainhill in 1829, Liverpool was one of the first towns to benefit from the rail-driven influx. Central Station, though, was a later addition to others in and around town. Opened in 1874 as a replacement for Brunswick Station, it was a handsome three-storey building, fronting Ranelagh Street. Despite being a busy place, it was closed under the Beeching cuts of the 1960s and demolished in 1973, leaving the underground low level service, begun in 1892, to continue unaccompanied.

### Did you know?

*The Liverpool and Manchester Railway was the first modern railway, in that both the goods and passenger traffic was operated by scheduled or timetabled locomotive hauled trains.*

**Right:** The Philharmonic Hall opened on Hope Street on 27 August, 1849. This provided the permanent base for the Liverpool Philharmonic Society that it had been seeking since it was founded in 1840. John Cunningham, a local architect, was commissioned to design the building. He started drawing up plans in 1844 for a concert room that would hold 1,500. However, his brief was extended later that year and he was instructed to widen his horizons and look to build a hall that could accommodate an audience of 2,100, along with space for a massive 250-strong orchestra, refreshment areas and spacious rest and robing rooms. Subscriptions from wealthy patrons were invited and prime seats sold in advance. The foundation stone was laid in 1846 and the famous German composer Felix Mendelssohn invited to write a piece to be played on opening night. Sadly, he died before completing the work, but the music that was played on that first evening was rapturously received. The Times newspaper reported that the Philharmonic Hall was 'the finest and best adapted to music' its critic had ever come across. Seen here in its prime in the early 1900s, the Hall had a magnificent organ installed in 1930

at a cost of £2,000. The acoustics and majesty of the building caused renowned conductor Sir Thomas Beecham to remark that it was 'the finest in Europe'. It was tragically destroyed in a fire in July 1933. The replacement, designed by H J Rouse, was built on the site and opened on 19 June, 1939 with a concert conducted by Beecham.

## Did you know?

*The city is home to the oldest surviving professional symphony orchestra in the UK, the Royal Liverpool Philharmonic Orchestra.*

**Right:** The statue of Queen Victoria has seen times that are both joyous and sad from its position amidst the memorial to the mighty monarch. The Victoria Monument, in Derby Square, once the site of the city castle, was the most important sculpture created by local artist C J Allen. Built from Portland stone, there are a number of bronze figures that accompany the Queen. This gives the whole edifice a very busy appearance, with four groups of three figures at

the base, four upper figures each with two infants and an angel at the summit. The unveiling took place on 27 September, 1906, and the ceremony was conducted by Princess Louise, Duchess of Argyll. She was Victoria and Albert's sixth child. A keen fitness fanatic, she often told her friends that she would outlive them all. That she lived to be 91 tends to support her statement! She died not long after the outbreak of World War II.

## Did you know?

*Liverpool has a greater number of public sculptures than any other location in the UK aside from Westminster and more Georgian houses than the City of Bath.*

**Left:** At the turn into the last century, this educational establishment was still something of a 'babe in arms'. Founded in 1881 as University College Liverpool, the first students were admitted the following year. In 1884, it became part of the federal group of seats of learning known as Victoria University that encompassed several northern colleges that included Manchester and Leeds. The grouping was shortlived as each sought its own identity and independence. Students had to be given external degrees from the University of London until Liverpool was finally afforded the right to award its own in 1903. Along with Leeds and Manchester, it was one of the six referred to as 'redbrick universities' by the snooty ancient universities in an attempt to devalue their standing. Bristol, Birmingham and Sheffield were the others to make up the sextet, but they all achieved good reputations as the years progressed and became centres of excellence in their own right. Even before getting its royal charter, our university had made its mark on the world. In 1894, one of its professors, Oliver Lodge, made the world's first public radio transmission and, two years later, took the United Kingdom's first surgical X-ray. The University of Liverpool can now boast nine Nobel prize winners among its alumni.

**Below:** Any Town Hall should represent the quality and nature of the place it serves. Ours is grand and imposing, setting just the right tone for one of Britain's premier cities. Situated on High Street, at the junction with Dale Street, Castle Street and Water Street, it is the most magnificent example of 18th century municipal architecture you could ever wish to come across. The late Georgian style of decoration is a delight and the suite of civic rooms must be the finest you could experience. Designed by John Wood as a replacement for a nearby earlier building, it was five years in construction before opening in 1754. An extension was added in 1785, but the main body was destroyed in a fire 10 years later. The hall was largely rebuilt and the dome added. It was not long after the centenary of this reconstruction that the photograph was taken. In the century and more since, further restoration was required after bomb damage in the last war, with additional works taking place in the 1990s.

### Did you know?

There are over 2,500 listed buildings in Liverpool, of which 27 are Grade I listed and 85 are Grade II*.

**Right:** The Empire Theatre that can be seen today, opened on 9 March, 1925, with a production of 'Better Days', starring Stanley Lupino, Maisie Gay and Ruth French. It was designed by W. and T. R. Milburn and was built by Moss Empires on the site of the former New Prince of Wales Theatre and Opera House which opened in 1866 and at the time was Liverpool's largest theatre. But it was only about three-quarters of the size of the existing Empire and was lit by gas and all the stage machinery was controlled by steam power. Within a year it was renamed the Royal Alexandra Theatre and Opera House to honour the Princess of Wales. The Empire Theatre that stands today was entirely rebuilt and enlarged in 1925 to become the most up to date theatre in the provinces. It had the widest auditorium in Europe, and with seating capacity of 2,381 is the largest two-tier theatre in the country.

**Left:** Wellington's Column or the Waterloo Memorial is a monument on the corner of William Brown Street and Lime Street. Designed by George Anderson Lawson, of Glasgow, and built between 1861 and 1865, it stands 40.2m (132ft) high. It reputedly weighs over 5 tonnes and was built to commemorate the victories of Arthur Wellesley, 1st Duke of Wellington, who won many battles during the Napoleonic Wars. The bronze figure of Wellington is perched on a fluted Doric sandstone column which in turn rests on a raised sandstone plinth. The four sides of the plinth contain bronze reliefs, one of which depicts a battle scene. It is flanked by two others which list Wellington's famous victories. The fourth panel simply has Wellington's

name. It was handed over to the Mayer of Liverpool by Mr John Torr, a local MP and secretary of the Monument Committee.

**Above:** Designed by local architects Cornelius Sherlock and H.H. Vale, the Walker Art Gallery was opened on 6 September, 1877, by the 15th Earl of Derby. It is named after its founding benefactor, Sir Andrew Barclay Walker, a former mayor of Liverpool and wealthy brewer. He was born in Ayrshire and expanded the family business to England and moved to live in Gateacre. In 1893 the Liverpool Royal Institution placed its collection on long-term loan to the gallery and in 1948 presented William Roscoe's collection and other works. This occurred during post-war reconstruction when the gallery was closed, re-opening in 1951. During the Second World War the gallery was taken over by the Ministry of Food and the collection was dispersed for safety. Extensions to the gallery were opened in 1884 and 1933 (following a two-year closure) when the gallery re-opened with an exhibition including Picasso and Gauguin. In 2002 the gallery re-opened following a major refurbishment. In 1986, the gallery achieved national status, as part of the National Museums and Galleries on Merseyside.

## Did you know?

*The first British Nobel Prize was awarded in 1902 to Ronald Ross, for his work on malaria. He was a professor at the Liverpool School of Tropical Medicine, the first school of its kind in the world.*

**This page:** Standing on St James' Mount in the city centre, the Cathedral Church of Christ in Liverpool, to give the Anglican cathedral its official title, has a commanding presence. It is the largest one in Britain, as befits the size of the diocese. Yet, in 1880 when JC Ryle was installed as the first Bishop of Liverpool, the rather plain St Peter's Parish Church acted as a substitute. After much verbal argy-bargy, church and civic leaders decided in 1902 that a competition should be held to find an architect and builder to create an appropriate centre of worship for the diocese. By this time, Bishop Ryle had died and Francis Scott were selected. He would later find more fame as the designer of the Post Office's red telephone boxes. The foundation stone was laid by King Edward VII in 1904 and the first element of the cathedral opened in 1910. The cathedral was not consecrated until 1924 and work continued on and off for years. The tower was not completed until 1942 and spiralling costs and other demands on the purse strings meant that the whole project was not finished until 1978. How often this baptismal font had been used in the meantime is a matter of guesswork.

## Did you know?

*Liverpool's Anglican Cathedral is the largest cathedral in Britain and the fifth largest in the world and has the tallest tower you can climb up in the UK, only Notre Dame Cathedral has more steps.*

Chavasse was in his place and he was involved in receiving over 100 applications for architectural consideration. The construction of such a mighty place of worship was so prestigious that the likes of the fabled Charles Rennie Mackintosh and Charles Herbert Reilly made submissions. Surprisingly, the plans of a 22-year-old student, George Gilbert

Britannic. Around it are three of the city's architectural losses. To the left, are The Goree Warehouses, built in 1793, and named after a slave embarkation island off Senegal, West Africa, which also gave its name to the adjacent road by St Nicholas's Church, known as Goree Piazza. The warehouses were demolished in 1958 following extensive Second World War bomb damage. Their site is now part of the Strand, which was widened in the Sixties as part of an ambitious scheme for an inner motorway around the city centre. In front of them runs the Liverpool Overhead Railway that was demolished within a few years of the Goree. The church in the background is St George's in Derby Square, which only just lasted to the end of the nineteenth century before demolition. Mann Island was formed in the 18th and 19th centuries as

**This page:** It is not difficult to 'spot the difference' between these two rare photographs from the area referred to as Mann Island. The top photograph dates from pre-1893, when the Liverpool Overhead Railway was opened. The photograph directly above, from about 1898, can be placed immediately because of the presence of the White Star offices, which opened in 1897. The White Star Line, was a prominent British shipping company, today most famous for its ill-fated vessel, the RMS Titanic, and the World War I loss of her sister ship,

part of the Liverpool dock complex. It was a virtual island, with Georges Dock to the north, Canning Dock to the east and south, and the River Mersey to the west. It was connected to the shoreline by a narrow neck of land opposite James Street. The site ceased to be an "island" in 1899 when the George's Dock was filled in to provide building land for the Port of Liverpool Building, and it became physically joined to the Pier Head. However, the name was continued in the roadway that extended into the Pier Head from James Street.

The growth of the American economy after its independence from Britain fairly took off in the early 19th century. With the rise in the volume of trade we had with 'the colonials', Liverpool's capacity as a port was rapidly expanded. New docks on the Mersey opened in quick succession in the 1830s and 1840s. Docks were also opened on the other side of the estuary at Wallasey Pool. These were all brought under one authority in 1855 and, in 1857, the Mersey Docks and Harbour Board was founded. This organisation took control of all the associated property had was given the power to collect dues and administrate the docks in their entirety. The main buildings at the Pier Head in these photographs are often referred to as our very own 'Three Graces'. The Royal Liver building opened in 1911 for the assurance company of that name that was founded in 1850 to provide financial help to those who had lost a wage-earning relative. The famous Liver Birds that sit on top of it, watching both sea and city, are said to herald the end of Liverpool should they ever leave. The squat

shape of the Cunard Building was erected during World War I as the headquarters of the shipping line that, at that time, owned such ships as the Mauritania and Lusitania. The 1907 photograph shows George's Dock before it was filled in to provide a site for Cunard's offices. The Dock or Harbour Board Office makes up the third of the 'Graces'. It was built in an Edwardian Baroque style with a distinctive dome sitting on its top and opened in 1907.

St George's Hall is a building in Neo-classical style which first opened its doors to the public in 1854, over ten years after it was first commissioned. The architect Harvey Lonsdale Elmes (1814-47) won the competition to design the concert hall and the law courts, and then made a design to unite them both into one magnificent civic building. However, he died when he was only 34, and the work was subsequently completed by Robert Rawlinson and Charles Robert Cockerell. The site of the hall was formerly occupied by the first Liverpool Infirmary from 1749 to 1824. Triennial music festivals were held in the city but there was no suitable hall to accommodate them. Following a public meeting in 1836 a company was formed to raise subscriptions for a hall in Liverpool to be used for the festivals, and for meetings, dinners and concerts. Shares were made available at £25 each and by January 1837 £23,350 (£1,760,060 as of 2011), had been raised. In 1838 the foundation stone was laid to commemorate the coronation of Queen Victoria. In 1969 the architectural historian Nikolaus Pevsner expressed his opinion that it is one of the finest neo-Grecian buildings in the world. The Hall is now designated by English Heritage as a Grade I listed building.

**Below:** The Calderstones constitutes one of Britain's most important megalithic rock-art sites, dating to c.2,500 BC. All that remains are six sandstone blocks. They may once have formed part of a chambered tomb known as a passage grave decorated with rock art symbols including spirals, concentric circles, arcs, cup and ring marks and footprints. The stones were relocated by Joseph Need Walker during his ownership, becoming a gateway feature to the Calderstones estate. The stones are now housed in the Harthill Greenhouses in Calderstones Park, Allerton, having been moved in 1954, from their location in an enclosure just outside the park gates, to protect them from further weathering.

> *Did you know?*
>
> *The Calder Stones in South Liverpool are believed by some to be older than Stonehenge.*

**Right:** The present site for the museum building is on a street formerly known as Shaw's Brow opposite St. George's Hall, which was donated by local MP and merchant William Brown. As a result, the building would be known as the William Brown Library and Museum. Around 400,000 people attended the opening of the new building in 1860. In the late 19th century a competition to design a combined extension to the museum and college of technology was won by William Mountford. Following completion, the new college extension opened in 1901. As a consequence of heavy bombing during the blitz, much of the Museum's collection was moved to less vulnerable locations. In the early first decade of the 21st century the museum on William Brown Street, was again expanded, taking over the lower half of the extension. To better reflect its larger size, the museum was renamed 'World Museum Liverpool'.

**Below right:** Princes Avenue in Liverpool 8 was once a grand avenue of merchants' houses with a tree-lined park in the middle of the road. It was one of the most sought after addresses in the city as a desirable place to live. Many of the houses on Princes Avenue still retain their former grand architectural style, but unfortunately some became derelict and were demolished. Thankfully, this heritage has now been recognised and gradually a number are being restored. The statue of Hugh Stowell Brown (1823-86) honoured the pastor and social reformer who worked tirelessly to improve social conditions for the poor in Victorian times. Born on the Isle of Man, he came to the mainland as a teenager looking for work with the Ordnance Survey. He turned to the church for a vocation in the 1840s and became the minister at Liverpool's Myrtle Street Baptist Chapel. His down-to-earth preaching and interest in the welfare of the poor made him a popular and well respected local figure. Brown encouraged investment in the 'Workman's Bank', an organisation founded by the church that helped those of meagre means make modest savings. Three years after his death, this statue was erected in his honour on Myrtle Street. The Chapel closed in 1939 and was later demolished. The statue was moved to Princes Avenue in 1954.

### Did you know?

*The English Heritage National Register of Historic Parks describes Merseyside's Victorian Parks as collectively the "most important in the country".*

**Above:** Now then, all together – 'aw'. What a lovely set of innocent little kiddies. Pictured in Dingle about the start of the 20th century. They have all scrubbed up so well and just look at the finery of those marvellous hats and bonnets that most of the older girls are wearing. It must have been a very special occasion to get this sort of display. The likeliest reason is that this was the preamble to the Whit Walk. That annual display of religious affiliation was as much about showing off your best clothes as it was about allegiance to a particular brand of Christianity. Even those who had no more than a couple of shillings to rub together made sure that the children had something out of the ordinary in which to dress when they set off behind the church banner, with a marching band leading the way and altar boys and choristers looking angelic in their surplices and cassocks. Afterwards, it was round to see Auntie Flo and Uncle Horace as they would always have a cash present for the youngsters.

**Right:** Rodney Street was named for Baron Rodney, a naval commander in the American War of Independence who also led the Royal Navy to a victory over the French in 1782 at the Battle of the Saintes. This street was first developed into a housing area around the turn into the 19th century. Nicholas Monsarrat, the author of

'The Cruel Sea', was born in 1910 at 11 Rodney Street, and William Ewart Gladstone, a Victorian prime minister, had his birthplace at No 62. Upper Duke Street, to the left, was named for the Duke of Cumberland, the son of King George II and uncle to King George III. The royal connection was continued on 9 August, 1902, when King Edward VII was crowned in Westminster. His subjects proved their loyalty to him and his Queen, the former Princess Alexandra of Denmark, by celebrating with street parties and a variety of official balls, parades and stirring speeches. The coronation nearly did not take place. Originally scheduled for 26 June, the King fell seriously ill with appendicitis just two days before that date. This had, until recent developments in anaesthesia and antiseptics, been a condition with a high mortality rate. Happily, his operation was such a success that Edward was sitting up in bed smoking a cigar just 24 hours later! God did bless the King that day.

**Above:** King George V honoured our city with a visit in 1923. He was received in the town Hall and was accompanied, as was nearly always the case, by his wife, Queen Mary. She cut a commanding figure that was heightened by her remarkable choice of headgear. It was always flamboyant, ranging from large, plumed hats to tall, colourful toques. Originally Princess Mary of Teck, her family had German ancestry, but she was born in London and brought up there. Some suspicions about her loyalty to the United Kingdom when the 1914-18 War began were largely dispelled when she instituted an austerity drive at Buckingham Palace, where she rationed food, and visited wounded and dying servicemen in

hospital. The King and Queen's commitment to the land of their birth was underlined by the change of family name from Saxe Coburg and Gotha to Windsor in 1917. The King was no fool and was careful to court popularity, knowing the fate that had befallen the likes of his relatives Kaiser Wilhelm II and Tsar Nicholas II in being exiled or assassinated.

**Below:** At one point the Mersey Docks and Harbour Company freight railway totalled 104 miles (166 km) of rail line, with connections to many other railways. A section of freight rail line ran under the Liverpool Overhead passenger railway, with trains constantly crossing the Dock Road from the docks into the freight terminals. By 1962, the dock railway's final days, the Overhead Railway had been dismantled, leaving the line below exposed and quite clearly in the way of future plans to modernise the road. What an amazing sight it must have been – a steam engine being led along one of the city's main thoroughfares by a man with a flag. Today, only the Canada Dock branch line is used to serve the docks, using diesel locomotives.

**This page:** At the time of its construction Queensway Tunnel was the longest underwater tunnel in the world, a title it held for 24 years. On 18, July, 1934, over 200,000 people gathered at the Old Haymarket to watch King George V and Queen Mary officially open the tunnel. Among those chosen to welcome the Royal party were Lord Mayor Councillor John Strong, Sir Thomas White, Chair of the Joint Tunnel Committee, Lord Sefton and Chief Constable A.K. Wilson. Liverpool City Police Band provided the music. On arrival, the Royal Party was introduced to Birkenhead's oldest inhabitant, 102-year-old Sammual Gillingham. The party then went on to officially open Central Library on Borough Road, which replaced the old library, demolished to make way for the tunnel entrance. In 1971 the Kingsway Tunnel opened to relieve congestion.

At the time of its opening the Queensway Tunnel was hailed as one of the great engineering triumphs and was Britain's biggest single municipal enterprise. It cost £8million and employed 1,700 men in difficult working conditions under the river bed. Construction of the tunnel required the excavation of 1,200,000 tons of rock and gravel and the building of two miles of roadway using 82,000 tons of cast iron and 270,000 tons of concrete. Following the official opening the tunnel was opened for a celebratory walk, which 80,000 people took part in, experiencing the novelty of being under the river bed. In 1934 a walk through the tunnel cost 6d.

**Left:** As Princess Elizabeth, the next in line to the throne, our future Queen took her responsibilities seriously. Although only a youthful 22-year-old when she accepted the key to the Anglican Cathedral from 13-year-old chorister Jeffrey Holliday, she exuded a mixture of grace, elegance and poise that would stand her in good stead when in public life. This ceremony was conducted on 29 March, 1949, and was watched by the Duke of Edinburgh who stood, as always, a couple of steps behind her. They had come to perform the official opening of the Cathedral's Great Central Door. Large crowds thronged the station approach at Lime Street as the royal train arrived and the young couple passed many thousands of cheering locals who lined the streets to greet them. A reception was held at the Town Hall and they departed on the short journey to Manchester where, on the following day, they would take part in a civic tour and factory visit

**Below:** The little lad does not really know why he is clutching the union flag but in 1962 we were all true royalists and flocked in droves to see a real princess in the flesh. It was not the warmest of days so people were well wrapped up as a drop of rain or a chilly breeze was not going to stop them from greeting their special guest. Princess Alexandra was inspecting the guard of honour provided by the Deva cadets. She has represented the Queen on numerous occasions, acting as a Counsellor of State in Her Majesty's absence abroad. In addition, she has made many official visits overseas, often accompanied by her husband, Angus Ogilvy, whom she married on 24 April, 1963 in Westminster Abbey. HRH Princess Alexandra is the Queen's first cousin and daughter of Princess Marina, another popular figure in royal circles. As a young woman Princess Alexandra made sure that she would have a wider knowledge of the world than some of her peers had. On completing her education she took a nursing course at Great Ormond Street Hospital before starting to undertake official engagements.

---

### Did you know?

*The Royal Liver Building clock, the biggest in Britain, started at the moment of King George V's Coronation, 22 June, 1911.*

---

**Left:** Students still hold Rag Weeks when they organise activities to raise funds for charities and good causes. They might have originated in Victorian times when students took time off in order to collect 'rags' or clothes to give to the poor and needy. The word might also refer to 'ragging' or harassing passers-by until they stumped up a donation. It was a week in which substantial amounts were raised for charities and was one of the few occasions when gown met town. Quite often, a student body would kidnap a celebrity or captain of industry and hold that person until a ransom was paid to an appropriate charity. It was generally good natured, but one or two did get a little carried away and overstepped the mark. Universities and colleges produced Rag Mags that were booklets of saucy and non-pc jokes that invariably offended minorities or the straightlaced, but they got away with causing offence as it was all in a good cause. It is difficult to work out what this happy group playing ring-a-roses with a bobby on Church Street in 1936 was trying to achieve, but they probably had their collecting buckets close at hand. The policeman on traffic duty seems to be distracted from his work as the 6A tram sits waiting to complete its short journey into Lord Street and then a right turn into Castle Street.

**Below:** It was a time of austerity as we struggled to get back on our feet after the costly 1939-45 War. We were in hock to the Americans and would continue to be so for the rest of the century. Even at the time of this scene some things were still rationed. No wonder people asked, 'Who actually won the war?' At least we had something to celebrate and take our minds off things. Queen Elizabeth was about to be crowned officially as our monarch on 2 June, 1953, and the bunting was stretched across Pitt Street, just as in every similar spot in Britain. Union flags flew and the boat was pushed out to make the best decorations we possibly could. All communities held street parties and a great time was had by everyone. As they waited for the celebrations to begin, a group of kiddies showed just how inventive they could be. They had no need of computers and Playstations for their fun, nor did they disappear into solitary confinement for their entertainment. These children communicated with one another as they enjoyed themselves. A hole in the ground was the site of a kitchen they had constructed. A fireguard, little table and teapot only needed lashings of imagination to turn the whole thing into a land of make believe where anything was possible.

## *Did you know?*

*In 1909 Eleanor Rathbone became the first ever women to be elected to Liverpool City Council. She was an independent MP and long-term campaigner for women's rights.*

**Above**: Some old-timers still refer to it as Speke Airport. Of course, its official name is now Liverpool John Lennon Airport. The majority of locals enjoy seeing the name of one of their own being used to identify it, just as those in Belfast support the use of George Best as a title. Back in 1946, Lennon was in infant school when these Dragon Rapides stood across from the control tower. These De Havilland planes were perhaps the most successful British built short-haul commercial passenger aircraft of the pre-war era. Sited in the grounds of Speke Hall, the airport hosted its first commercial flights in 1930 and developed a particularly lucrative trade crossing the Irish Sea. It was taken over by the RAF during World War II and Rootes built many bomber planes here while Lockheed used the airport to assemble Hudsons and Mustangs shipped in from the United States. Civil aviation resumed after the war, but it was not until the city assumed control for its operation in 1961 that it could start to develop into the international terminal it is today. It took on its current name in 2002.

### Did you know?

*The first package holiday flight departed from Liverpool (Speke) Airport in 1952.*

**Left:** Marking 60 years since Liverpool Corporation formed its own tramway company, the very last journey was made by car 293 on 14 September, 1957. Large crowds witnessed its final departure from the Pier Head and many people lined the route all the way to the Edge Lane Depot. They feted the vehicle that was one of those that had given such good service over the years. During that final week special commemorative tickets went on sale, some of which were hoarded by collectors of memorabilia and fans of the tram system. In 1958, car 293 was shipped to the Seashore Trolley Museum in Maine, USA, where it remains, though in a deteriorated condition. Most historians agree that the first tramway was created in New York by John Stevenson, a young Irish immigrant. He had a coach building business and founded a company to lay tracks on which horse drawn vehicles could move. He opened his Harlem and New York Railroad in late 1832 and helped begin a transport revolution. When Liverpool electrified its routes at the end of the 19th century the attraction of this form of conveyance was immediately obvious. In 1901, over 100 million passenger journeys were made as the service was embraced as a marvel of the 20th century.

**Above:** In nonchalant pose, three of the Beatles, John, Ringo and George, make a phone call during the filming of 'A Hard Day's Night'. For the occasion London's Marylebone Station became Liverpool's Lime Street Station. This 1964 British musical comedy was at the height of Beatlemania and first film to star the group. Paul is not in shot, as he is waiting in the station in a disguise.

## *Did you know?*

*The Beatles' "Yesterday" is the most covered song in history, appearing in the Guinness Book of Records with over three thousand recorded versions.*

*According to EMI, the Beatles have sold an estimated one billion media (records, tapes, CD's) worldwide making them the best-selling musical group of all time.*

The 1966 World Cup football championship was held in England. In Claudia Street, near Goodison Park ground where some of the matches were played, neighbours made paper flowers from red, white and blue crepe paper. Kerbstones were painted and windows were decorated. The Brazilians had arrived and this was the tribute to the world champions from thousands of soccer fans who have had their own taste of greatness in recent years. Who will ever forget the world cup final when the England side became legends beating West Germany 4-2 at Wembley. How long will it be before we get the chance we deserve to host the finals again?...when the day eventually arrives it may be the best chance we have of becoming world champions again.

# Halewood International Ltd
## The Drinks are On Us

In just over thirty years Halewood International Ltd has gone from being a Yorkshire-based startup company to become the UK's largest independent drinks manufacturer and distributor. Today it has a turnover in excess of £250 million, and more than 1,500 employees worldwide.

The business which became Halewood International was founded by visionary entrepreneur John Halewood in 1978, although the company name in those early days was Halewood Vintners Limited.

Since its inception the company has grown and thrived on innovation, creativity and energy, and more than three decades on, John Halewood's passion and enthusiasm for the business remains undiminished in his current role as the company's Chief Executive and major shareholder.

It is this passion and vision, combined with the wide-ranging talents of staff and management, that have helped this Liverpool company attain its current position manufacturing and distributing some of the UK's best known alcoholic drinks brands from Lambrini to Lamb's Navy Rum, from Tsingtao Chinese Beer to Crabbie's Alcoholic Ginger Beer, from Red Square Vodka to Reloaded and fine wines.

The Group portfolio currently spans wines and wine-style drinks, beers and ciders, spirits and speciality and ready to drink (RTD) products. But success in the UK is only half the story.

From its headquarters at the Sovereign Distillery in Wilson Road, the company controls operations in South Africa, Romania and China, and as well as manufacturing its own brands and products the company is able to offer the drinks industry some of the most sophisticated packaging and production facilities in the UK on a contract basis.

John Halewood started his working life in the Liverpool drinks trade, working for a local company – Hall & Bramley Ltd. 'H&B' had been founded in 1860 by prominent local businessman Charlton R Hall. By 1892 the firm was based in Orange Street and was one of the most noted wholesale wine and spirit houses in the city. On the founder's death in 1900 his son Charlton Hall junior took into partnership William Foulkes and JT Bramley. Hall & Bramley became a limited company in 1910 when two senior staff, Harold Roughsedge and George Coonan acquired a major stake in the firm: they, and their sons, would run the firm for many decades thereafter. The firm eventually relocated to the Racecourse Industrial estate at Aintree.

*Top left: Founder John Halewood.* **Above:** *Staff outside the company's Kirkby premises in the early years.* **Left and below:** *Views inside Halewood International in the 1980s.*

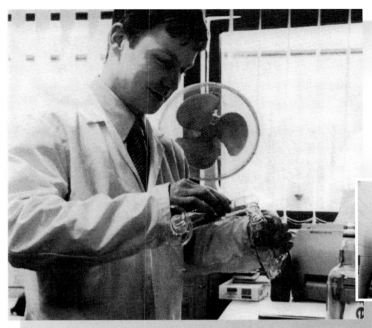

Despite Liverpool being Halewood's home the genesis of the business took place in West Yorkshire, the area where John Halewood was living whilst he worked for Gonzalez Byass, a sherry shipper.

Having seen an opportunity to 'do his own thing' John started by using the garage at his home for storing cases of wine and delivering them himself. This soon changed to a separate 'lock-up', from where further larger premises were soon acquired, incorporating office accommodation, storage facilities and the building of a winery to produce British wine.

Because of John's early involvement with sherry it was only natural that he had 'kicked off' the business with a sherry-type product, Montilla, which although not a fortified wine has a very similar style to sherry, and indeed Amontillado (a style of Sherry) means Montilla-like.

Throughout its history H&B provided training for many young men in the trade. None was more notable than John Halewood - although John recalls that his own 'training' amounted to no more than being given six bottles of sherry, car keys, a price list and a map of Yorkshire. In 1997 he returned to buy the firm during a period of rapid expansion of his Halewood Group.

John was born on the Wirral, in Wallasey, to an Irish mother, Eileen, and a father who was a Naval Officer and Engineer. Both helped John when he eventually set up his own business as a 'one-man band'. John's mother Eileen Halewood was a Director and shareholder of the business until her death, aged 87, in 2010.

Although the business has grown organically, strategic purchases have also been a feature of the development, with two other Merseyside businesses being absorbed along the way: John Buccleugh, which was based in Kirkby, (to be more precise it was the equipment that was situated at John Buccleugh's in Kirkby which was bought by Halewood International, not the business), and Lamb & Watt, a Warrington-based drinks company founded as long ago as 1847.

The development of his British Winery was the first opportunity that John Halewood had to produce products 'in house'; but because of the lack of any bottling capacity the finished wine had to be moved in bulk, taken to be bottled in Kirkby prior to most of it being shipped back to Yorkshire for storage and distribution. This was obviously not an ideal situation. (It was at this time that products such as Copperfield British Sherry and Mansion House British Sherry were introduced into the market, and gained rapid distribution in sales).

**Top left:** *Liquid development.* **Above:** *Roberttown Tank Farm.* **Left:** *Eileen Halewood.* **Below:** *John Halewood in the dark shirt at Gonzalez Byass in 1970, with Ken Brown, who runs the Halewood Scottish office today, standing behind over John's right shoulder.*

Subsequent European legislation, however, meant that products such as these could not continue to be called British Sherry, but had to be re-described as Fortified British Wine.

During this period the sales force began to expand - originally the 'sales force' was simply John Halewood himself – along with finance and administration staff supporting the sales staff's efforts.

In the 1980s Halewood purchased what is the oldest wine merchant in the United Kingdom, Chalié Richards & Company, which was founded in St. James's in London in 1700 and over the years received a number of Royal Warrants.

The history of Chalié Richards began in 1685 when the Chalié family fled from Montauban to Holland after the revocation of the Edict of Nantes in 1685. Brothers James and John, already connected with the wine trade, soon came to London and established the business of 'Wine Merchants, General Merchants and Bankers'. They took premises in Mincing Lane and had their cellars next door under the Clothworkers Hall. Their wine business grew rapidly, and gained the reputation of 'One of the finest corners of the metropolis'. Anecdotes abound concerning famous or aristocratic customers whose ability to order wines far exceeded their ability to pay. The playwright Richard Brinsley Sheridan was one such customer, with apparently a good taste in Burgundy, Port and old Hock. A shipping record of 1785 shows that, out of a total of 1,423 hogsheads of Claret shipped to London, Chalié shipped 295, more than twice as many as any other trader. In the early nineteenth century, Matthew Chalié (son of James) was joined by William Parry Richards. With Richards' arrival began a tradition of royal patronage, which was to last well over a century. In fact, the house of Chalié was to supply the six successive monarchs from George IV through to George VI. In 1820 five pipes of Port were delivered to

Carlton Palace 'for the use of His Majesty'. In 1837, the year of accession of Queen Victoria, one of the first acts performed by her Lord Steward was the appointment of Matthew Chalié as purveyor of wines and spirits to Her Majesty. By the end of the century, Chalié Richards and Company, as it had become known, had moved into large and spacious premises at 4 Pall Mall East, and maintained magnificent cellars in the Strand, within the royal precinct of the Savoy. A century later the role of wine shippers has been revived under the patronage of John Halewood as the 'fine wine' arm of the Halewood Group, selling wine which it either owns or through agency arrangements from around the world.

This range includes the highly successful One World range, which is the generic name covering wines from Australia, South Africa, California, Italy, New Zealand and Romania, with each country having its own sub-brand, Ocean Point from Australia for example .

In addition to alcoholic products, Chalié is also the brand owner of Eisberg the brand leading de-alcoholised wine – an ideal alternative for people who enjoy the taste and style of wine, but who for whatever reason – perhaps expectant mothers or designated drivers – choose not to drink at that particular time.

*Top left: Staff pictured outside their premises in Roberttown, c.1990.* **Above left:** *Chalié Richards advertising.* **Above:** *An aerial view of Halewood International, Huyton.* **Below:** *Lloyds Bank Management and three-time Grand National winner Red Rum pictured outside Halewood International, Huyton, in 1994.*

Another important purchase was of the Rowley Wine Company in 1992, enabling the business to move into production of its own still and carbonated drinks, especially perries. With total control of production, Halewood was able to expand both its branded product range as well as offering "own label" facilities.

As bottling took place in Merseyside, it made sense to look to relocate the business in that area. In 1993 the present Halewood site in Huyton was purchased (or rather part of what is the present site), half of it originally being occupied by a beer distribution operation.

The move to Liverpool saw the development of what became Halewood's largest brand, Lambrini. Although this wasn't the first of the Halewood products to receive television support it was certainly the first to receive national advertising support, along with poster and radio advertising. Today Lambrini is one of the largest brands in the take-home market. At this time Red Square Vodka was also developed into a leading brand vodka along with its ready to drink (RTD) flavoured counterparts.

Wines from Eastern Europe have featured significantly in the development of the Halewood Group. John Halewood was one of the first shippers of Bulgarian wine into the United Kingdom, and achieved early distribution through Asda supermarkets. However, because competition sprang up from the Bulgarian state, which didn't seem to understand the concept of profitability, John Halewood moved his interests to Romania.

Despite the difficulty in doing business with a Communist state (during Ceausecu's regime), John was still able to build a significant volume of business bringing Romanian wines into the U.K., and indeed at one time sales exceeded one million 9-litre cases.

With the fall of communism in 1989, Halewood along with Pernod Ricard and a German wine importer, formed the first joint venture between western and Romanian companies. Since then Halewood has bought land and developed vineyards in all the key growing areas, as well as developing some of the wineries into tourist attractions.

Within a decade the Group had founded its first Romanian subsidiary, and in so doing became the largest exporter of Romanian wines to Britain. After investing more than $10 million, the Halewood Group now owns three subsidiaries in

*Top left:* Halewood International's Lambrini, one of the largest brands in the take-home market. *Above:* Halewood's wine estate and vineyards in the Delau Mare region of Romania. *Below:* Sales team at the sparkling wine facility in Azuga (Transylvania), Romania, 2004.

Romania - in wine growing, wine making and wine distribution – and has more than 200 employees. The Group manages over 400 hectares of vines in three major wine areas: Dealu Mare, Podisul Transilvaniei and Murfatlar. The average annual wine production is 42,000 hl and the storage capacity is 90,420 hl.

Halewood Romania is one of the key wine agency companies in that country.

Meanwhile, a South African business, Oasis Breweries, was something of a 'basket case' when it was acquired in 1999. In the last few years, however, its fortunes have been turned round via strategic investment and a professional and dedicated management team.

Although not part of the Halewood Holdings Group, John Halewood also owns a drink packaging business in Chorley – H&A Prestige Packaging – and has a shareholding in something completely unconnected with the drinks industry, HIFX – Halewood International Foreign Exchange – based in Windsor.

Despite all the international connections (which also includes a business in China) the majority of Halewood's business is in the United Kingdom, supplying all major retailers and wholesalers as well as specialist wine

and spirit and convenience stores. Structural changes now underway mean that in future much greater emphasis will be placed on developing international business by building strategic partnerships with distribution companies based in target export territories.

*Top left:* A bird's eye view of Halewood International's South Africa head office. *Above:* A view inside the factory today. *Left:* A selection of Halewood International products. *Below:* Linus van Zyl, Sales Director, Kevin Pillay, Senior Financial Manager and Mike Veysie, Managing Director of Halewood International South Africa.

Crabbie's and the local community the Crabbie's brand sponsors the 'Hibs' Football Club.

With Halewood interests growing internationally, the Group now employs around 1,500 people, of which around 350 are based in Liverpool.

Meanwhile, when not planning and discussing new ideas, which includes developing interesting label designs, unique bottle shapes and the next flavour to catch the consumer's attention and imagination, John Halewood's other passion is horse racing. His horse 'Amberleigh House' trained by Ginger McCain, who had successfully trained 'Red Rum', won the 2004 Aintree Grand National. John currently has 15 horses in training.

Bringing the portfolio up to date, Crabbie's Alcoholic Ginger Beer, launched in February 2009, has been the most successful product launch that the Group has ever enjoyed. It has benefited from significant advertising support from quirky television and radio advertising to posters and the purchase of a London Routemaster bus, heavily branded, which can be used for trade show events - it was used at the Scottish Open Golf Championship for example, and it is kitted out to show video presentations as well as offering on-board tastings.

The original Crabbie's Ginger Wine had been in the company portfolio for some time. John Crabbie & Co was established in 1801 in Leith in Scotland. To maintain the connection between

*Top left:* A double decker bus advertising Crabbie's Alcoholic Ginger Beer. *Left:* John Halewood lifts the winning owner plate when the company's horse 'Amberleigh House' won the 2004 Martell Grand National. *Left inset:* John Halewood pictured with Amberleigh House after his triumph. *Above:* The Lambrini-Lambanana and the Crabbie's Elephant with artist, Sophie Green on left and Al Cross and Sue Beck, brand managers for Crabbie's and Lambrini.

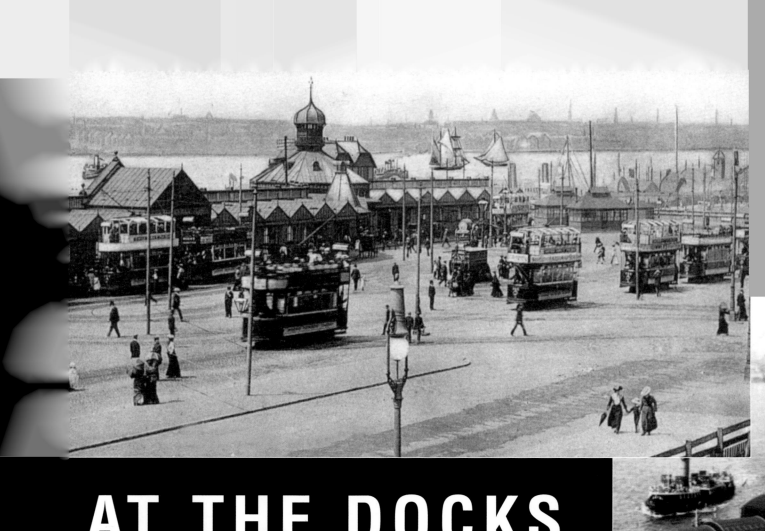

# AT THE DOCKS

This trio of photographs of the Pier Head shows how its face changed over half a century from the early 1900s through to the 1950s. It can trace its history to the action of monks from Birkenhead Priory establishing a ferry service across the river in the early 13th century, though there were no docks or formal landing area here at that time. It was with the introduction of steamboats over 600 years later that the need for a proper landing stage, to be known as Pier Head, was created. The first floating one was built in 1847, with Princes Stage being added a decade later. By 1876, the small stage at Pier Head had been extended to a degree that it had become the longest of its type in the world and was regularly serving thousands of workers and commuters making their way across the river or down the coast to their places of employment. Princes Stage was attracting the custom of large Cunard and White Star liners. A dredging programme was begun in the 1890s that helped large vessels get closer to shore, doing away with the need to use smaller craft to transfer passengers to and from land. During the last century, the Pier Head served as both a tram and bus interchange, but from the 1950s onwards its influence and importance began to wane as the great ocean-going liners went elsewhere.

**Above:** The waterfront has always been restricted to the people of Liverpool and the first view taken in 1911 shows a scene that would have been enclosed by storage sheds along the Dock Road. Eagle-eyed readers will notice the Liver Building in the background minus its Liver birds.

### Did you know?

*For periods during the 19th century the wealth of Liverpool exceeded that of London and Liverpool's Custom House was the single largest contributor to the British Exchequer.*

**Left and above:** The aerial view of the Customs House was taken in 1936, but the other scene that includes the pump house at Albert Dock is probably from well over 50 years earlier. The distinctive domed building is part of the city's lost architectural heritage. It was built between 1828 and 1839 by the town architect, John Foster, on the site of the original Old Dock. As well as dealing with the collection of duties and overseeing the import and export of goods, the building complex contained a post office and telegraph station in addition to providing accommodation for the Mersey Docks and Harbour Board. It was the fourth such Customs House to be built in this vicinity and provided good service for over 100 years. In the fantastic picture above, the Overhead Railway bisects this view from left to right and many readers will remember the marvellous rooftop views this provided. You may also recognise Canning Dock on the left of shot and Salthouse to the right. Readers may also be able to pick out the Maritime Museum and Granada Television Studios. In the foreground is Albert Dock, which has become a major tourist attraction in its own right.

**Above and below:** The crowded steamers by the landing stages show just how popular they were to Merseysiders in providing frequent and reliable transport across to Birkenhead in the days before the road tunnels under the river were constructed. The Royal Liver building officially appeared on the waterfront at the Pier Head when Lord Sheffield presided at an opening ceremony on 19 July, 1911. This was just over three years after the foundation stone was laid. From that evidence and knowing that these photographs were taken in early 1909 and 1912 respectively we can tell which is which. In the earlier one it seems odd to look across the water and not see a Liver Bird high on its resting place. The Royal Liver building stands

**Below:** The Mersey has provided Liverpool with a source of lifeblood ever since the first settlement was made here. Reference to the name that means 'muddy pool' was made in the 12th century and King John declared the place a borough in 1207. In earlier days the tides, gales and rainy weather would have been too much for the Romans who preferred to visit this part of the coastline in the gentler spring and summer. There continued to be little in the way of population growth until Thomas Steers built several docks and a pier in the early 1700s. Coal, textiles and salt could be brought down the river from Lancashire and Cheshire and goods imported from the rapidly expanding United States and the West Indies. The wide and sheltered estuary provided easy and comparatively safe access for merchant ships and, as passenger traffic took on an importance, great liners were able to make use of the port. The river starts to widen from the Runcorn Gap into an estuary that is some three miles in width, though it narrows to less than one mile in the stretch between the city and Birkenhead. It is across this part that the famous Mersey Ferry, immortalised in song in the mid 1960s by Gerry Marsden, has plied a trade in one form or another for hundreds of years.

nearly 300 feet above the river and was the tallest structure in the city at the time of its opening. It was one of the first in the world to be made from reinforced concrete. Its clock faces are larger than those of Big Ben, thus making them the largest electronically driven clocks in the country. The building is still the headquarters of the Royal Liver Assurance Company. The renowned Liver Birds were designed by Carl Bernard Bartels and provided the title of a popular TV sitcom of the 1970s, written by Carla Lane and Myra Taylor, then two Liverpool housewives.

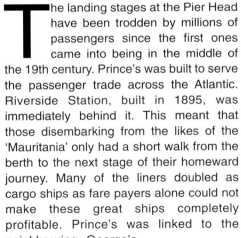

The landing stages at the Pier Head have been trodden by millions of passengers since the first ones came into being in the middle of the 19th century. Prince's was built to serve the passenger trade across the Atlantic. Riverside Station, built in 1895, was immediately behind it. This meant that those disembarking from the likes of the 'Mauritania' only had a short walk from the berth to the next stage of their homeward journey. Many of the liners doubled as cargo ships as fare payers alone could not make these great ships completely profitable. Prince's was linked to the neighbouring George's stage in the 1870s and extended, making it the world's longest floating stage at that time. As evidenced here, coastal packets and ocean going steamers crowded along the front in a seemingly never ending stream of vessels plying their trade in what was once one of the most important ports on the globe. This was one of the most significant of British maritime landmarks as the landing stage and the wooden decking were crossed by thousands on a daily basis. These people, whether visitors, workers or those heading off to America or across to the Isle of Man and Ireland, were central to the success of our city. The popular folk song, 'Leaving of Liverpool' begins with the lines, 'Farewell to Prince's landing stage, River Mersey fare thee well', telling of feelings of one such passenger who is bound for California on the clipper 'Davy Crockett'.

## Did you know?

The World's first scheduled transatlantic passenger service (wooden paddle-streamer's) set sail from Liverpool to Halifax, Nova Scotia, in 1840. Owned by Samuel Cunard the ships carried 115 passengers in conditions that Charles Dickens unfavourably likened to a "gigantic hearse".

**Below:** Looking down on the South Docks from the Liver Building in the mid 1950s, we are viewing a moment during the time that Liverpool's dependence upon maritime trade of one sort or another was beginning to be questioned. The great liners failed to attract sufficient passengers to support their existence and work at the docks was harder to find. The docks were wound down in importance during the latter part of the 20th century at a quicker rate than they had arrived. With the opening up of trade with the new colonies and North America in the 1700s, pressure on our port became ever more intense. Ships could not stay afloat in safety and often had to be beached. It was no use anchoring large ships out in the river for their cargoes to be unloaded as changing tides, a strong current and an insufficient number of barges made this a difficult and dangerous task. The first dock was built in 1715, becoming known later as Old Dock and then Canning Dock. Salthouse and George's opened in 1753 and 1771 respectively. In the following century, dozens more opened on Merseyside. Inward trade traffic that had been measured in tens of thousands of tons grew to over 12 million by 1900. With competition from elsewhere, change in trade requirements and the advancement of technology, the need for these docks shrank and virtually disappeared. By the late 1970s we were looking at derelict buildings and waste land. In more recent times, much of dockland has been revitalised as a place for tourists to visit, into retail areas and apartment developments.

## Did you know?

*Ferries, railways, transatlantic steamships, municipal trams, electric trains and the helicopter were all pioneered in Liverpool as modes of mass transit.*

**Right:** If you are brave, or perhaps foolhardy, enough to have climbed to the top of one of the power station chimneys that towered above the waterfront on the site of the former Clarence Dock in 1952, then this is the scene you would have surveyed. There were eventually three chimneys serving the power station, with the last one being added to the 1937 complex about the time that this elevated picture was taken. They were known as either 'the three sisters' or 'the three ugly sisters', depending upon your architectural opinion. Clarence Dock was built to serve steamships at a spot separate from the main docks in case

sparks from these vessels caused damage to more inflammable sailing ships. It was named after the former Duke of Clarence who had become King William IV just a few months before the dock opened on 16 September, 1830. It ceased to be used after World War I and was filled in during the late 1920s, though the graving docks on which the power station was built were retained. Clarence Dock was situated along the route of the overhead railway, though it also had its own functioning trackway. It was largely used on the Irish routes and its importance in this role at the time of the potato famine of the mid 19th century is recalled in a plaque unveiled on the old dock gates in 2000. It reads 'Through these gates passed most of the 1,300,000 Irish migrants who fled from the Great Famine and took the ship to Liverpool in the years 1845-52'. The power station and its chimneys disappeared from view in the 1990s.

**Right:** A consignment of Leyland buses to New York for London Bus Week in 1952 caused quite a stir at the Docks. Some work has been done on the first vehicle; note that two windows are now missing from the lower deck (and perhaps the upper windows are missing too? Hard to tell...). A plywood cover has also been knocked together and placed across the doorway to prevent people from boarding the bus. One has to wonder about what took place to make the authorities suddenly think of covering up the door!

# GETTING AROUND

Here we have two scenes from the Victorian era. They both demonstrate the importance of the horse as a source of power and energy. This noble beast served its master on the land, pulling ploughs, dragging raw materials and carrying goods. It provided someone with a means of travel from A to B, either carrying an individual on its back or in front of a cart or carriage. When better roads were built through towns, both private and civic companies organised public transport of one sort or another. The first buses and trams that we used were pulled by horses. These new conveyances offered people an easy journey into and out of town. They also

meant that gardeners were thrilled to reach for buckets and shovels to collect the copious amount of manure that was deposited. The smell in town centres was not very pleasant, but at least the roses and rhubarb flourished. During the period represented in these scenes, you would have seen all manner of private vehicles that had dozens of styles and names to their designs. There were broughams and buggies, cabriolets and carioles and hackneys and hansoms. Some were practical and others chic, but they all had one common denominator: they relied on horse power. The tram proclaiming the merits of Brooke's soap was on Church Street about 1880, a couple of years after the Bon Marche building to the left was built. St Peter's Church on the right was demolished in the 1920s and was later used as a site by Top Shop. The omnibus with the advert for the overhead railway was passing William Truesdale's grocery business and the tobacconist's shop belonging to Elizabeth Handley in 1893. This was on Lark Lane, where we can also observe the premises of Arnold Thomas, a glass and china dealer, and a Wesleyan Chapel.

NOSTALGIC MEMORIES OF LIVERPOOL

**Above and bottom right:** In 1932, the No 10 tram on Lord Street, heading for Pier Head, was part of a fleet that enjoyed great popularity either side of the Great War. Liverpool Corporation began acquiring parts of the assets of the Liverpool United Tramways and Omnibus Company in the latter years of the 19th century. By the year of Victoria's Diamond Jubilee the takeover was virtually completed. The Liverpool Tramway Transfer Act of 1897 gave the green light for conversion from mechanical power to electricity and the modern tramway was born. The first electric car left Dingle in 1898 and by 1902 nearly every mile of track had been converted. The last horse drawn tram was seen in December 1902 and the cleaner, newer power now reigned supreme. Trams also had an effect on housing as they meant that people could move out of crowded areas to places with more space and cleaner living conditions and yet be able to access their workplaces quickly and cheaply. However, all good things come to an end and by the start of the 1950s, when the tram at Aigburth Vale was photographed, the end was nigh. On 14 September, 1957, the last tram (No 293) left the Pier Head for Bowring Park

on route 6A, returning to the Edge Lane depot. Regular passengers on this route were pupils from Aigburth Vale High school, which opened in 1909. Aigburth is mainly residential and covers an area following Aigburth Road (A561) and the areas either side of it, south of Sefton Park.

**Top right:** Lime Street is one of the oldest working stations in the world. It rightly holds something of a special place in the hearts of railway buffs and aficionados of the age of steam. This locomotive, impatiently waiting by the platform, was photographed about 1890. By then the station had been functioning for over 50 years. In the early days of the Liverpool and Manchester Railway, the terminus at our end was at Crown Street, Edge Hill. This opened in 1830, but work on the mighty Lime Street Station was begun three years later and it opened for business in 1836. With increased demand for this new form of public transport, it was soon necessary to extend the station. A single curved roof was built in 1849 and a second one added in the 1880s. This latter roofing, a massive mix of glass and iron, is still in place today.

**Did you know?**

In 1868, the Liverpool Tramways Act was passed authorising the laying of tramlines, the first in England to be authorised.

The first passenger-carrying hovercraft to enter service ran along the North Wales coast from Moreton to Rhyl in 1962.

**Above and below:** The No 86 bus to Garston was one of a fleet of AEC Regent III vehicles with Crossley bodies that was put into service by Liverpool Corporation in June 1953. So, all in the same month, we had a newly crowned Queen and a newly introduced omnibus. The Associated Equipment Company (AEC) built buses, coaches and lorries from 1912 until 1979. Perhaps the company's most famous model is the Routemaster, the double decker that is especially linked with use in London in the late 1950s and 1960s. The Regent pictured near the Pier Head was powered by a 9.6 litre diesel engine and used a Wilson pre-selective gearbox. The history of public transport on Merseyside dates back to the early 19th century when licensed horse drawn carriages were introduced. Larger vehicles, with wheels set on rails followed, and in 1876, the Liverpool United Tramways and Omnibus

Company was formed. The photograph of St Mary's Road, in Garston, shows that, in 1952, diesel engines still operated alongside electrically powered motors and would continue to do so for another five years until trams were mothballed. The No 82 bus is leading the way, turning into St Mary's Road from Church Road, on route to the Pier Head. The Liverpool Savings Bank building is still in place. Today, Garston is a major shipping and container port, second only to Liverpool Docks in the North-West. and is home to Liverpool South Parkway railway station, a major new interchange station which opened in 2007.

**Above:** At first glance this photograph could be from the 1800s. It is, however, from the 1980 'Rocket 150' celebration to mark the 150th Anniversary of the Rainhill trials. A replica of the Rocket was specially built for the event and can be seen here passing crowds of rail enthusiasts on the day. At the original trials, locomotives were run two or three per day, and several tests for each locomotive were performed over the course of several days, in order to establish the most efficient locomotive

for haulage on the Liverpool & Manchester Railway. The Rocket, designed by Robert Stephenson (1803-1859) and George Stephenson (1781-1848), was the only locomotive to complete the trials. It averaged 12 miles per hour (19 km/h), achieving a top speed of 30 miles per hour (48 km/h) hauling 13 tons, and was declared the winner of the £500 prize. The Stephensons were accordingly given the contract to produce locomotives for the Liverpool & Manchester Railway. The Rocket ran on the Liverpool and Manchester Railway from 1829 to 1836 and the Midgeholme Colliery Railway in County Durham between 1836 and 1840.

## Did you know?

*The first Steamroller in Britain was purchased by Liverpool City Council in 1867.*

# BIRD'S EYE VIEW

The overhead electric railway provided a grand way to see the sights of the city dockland. It was often the sort of a treat that grandpa would give us by taking us on a ride and providing us with an ice cream to enjoy at the same time. Youngsters thrilled at getting such a privileged view of the great ocean-going liners that came to call, especially either side of the last war. Nicknamed 'The Dockers' Umbrella', the railway was the first of its type in the world. It was also the first to use automatic signalling and electric lights. It ran from Alexandra Dock to Herculaneum Dock and was opened on 4 February, 1893, by the Marquis of Salisbury. By the end of 1896 the route had been extended to Dingle and Seaforth. The purpose-built trains were unique as they required no locomotive to pull them along the rails. The popular railway flourished for over 60 years, but in time the corrugated iron decking on which the tracks were laid became badly corroded. The owners looked to the City Council and Harbour Board for financial help in making expensive repairs, but to no avail. Among howls of protest from those who treasured the overhead railway, it ran its last train on 30 December, 1956. To the right, the St Nicholas' Church was damaged in the Second World War, but was later restored successfully.

### Did you know?

*In 1897, the Lumiére brothers filmed Liverpool, including what is believed to be the world's first tracking shot, taken from the Liverpool Overhead Railway – the first elevated electrified railway.*

**Below:** The modern finger of the incongruous ventilation shaft for St John's Market was nearing completion in 1967. It was to become the second tallest free standing structure in the city and has been the subject of controversy ever since it began to appear on the skyline. It was opened by the Queen in 1969, but never used for its original purpose. St John's Beacon, as it was then known, became something of a novelty with a revolving restaurant near the top, above which there was an observation post from where visitors could gaze across the city or down towards the toll booths at the Queensway entrance to the Mersey Tunnel in the foreground of this picture. The 558 steps up the staircase were a daunting prospect for those not in the fittest of condition, so it was a pair of speedy lifts that got the greatest use. Health and safety problems led to the closure of the restaurant in 1977. This reopened in 1983, but was unsuccessful and the beacon lay empty and derelict for the rest of the century. It was refurbished in 2000 and turned into offices and a transmitting station for Radio City.

## Did you know?

*The Aintree Grand National was first run in 1839 and the famous four-and-a-half mile marathon now attracts an estimated 500 to 600 million viewers in over 140 countries worldwide. The first five Grand Nationals included one jump that was a stone wall. It was situated where the water jump now stands.*

**This page:** The trio of trams headed down Water Street in 1946, away from the Royal Liver building in the distance and on to Dale Street. They were approaching the Town Hall that was the centre of civic and commercial business in late Georgian and early Victorian times. The frieze around the outside, illustrating Liverpool's trading routes, includes lions, crocodiles, elephants and African faces. The impressive Barclays Bank was built next to the Town Hall in 1927 as the head office of Martin's Bank, which incorporated Heywood's Bank. Heywood's was founded by Arthur and Benjamin Heywood, who owned slaving vessels. Water Street is on one of the city's oldest streets that was the main approach up from the river's shoreline where travellers would have disembarked in the past from ferries out of Birkenhead or sailing boats from Ireland. It was once known as Bonk Street, the first word being local dialect for 'river bank'. Many merchants had handsome homes and offices built on Water Street. The gentleman in the picture below from Water Street in the 1920s appears to be posing for the camera alongside his works vehicle.

The Coronation Gardens were created from a bomb site on the edge of Paradise Street. Named for that eventful day in the summer of 1953 when Queen Elizabeth was crowned, the lawns, flower beds and park benches provided a pleasantly calm and green oasis not far from the heart of the city. Perhaps those sitting in the sunshine had been among the lucky people who managed to view the scenes at Westminster Abbey on television. This was the occasion that prompted many to go out and buy their first tv set. St John's Gardens, on William Brown Street, have happily survived the demands of the developers and remain somewhere locals can escape from the hurly burly of city life for a while. It is a good place for office workers to unpack a few sandwiches at lunchtime and know that they can look at grass, plants and trees instead of a computer screen. The park takes its name from the church that stood here until 1887 and was laid out by Thomas Shelmerdine, opening in 1904. It was primarily intended as a place to exhibit public art and there are many monuments within its grounds that are the work of some of the most eminent sculptors of the late Victorian and Edwardian period. Most of the figures on the monuments are of people who were social reformers or great philanthropists. So, as well as enjoying a break from work, visitors can brush up on their history at the same time.

## Did you know?

*In 1943, Richard Burton made his first professional stage appearance at the Royal Court Theatre in Liverpool, in The Druid's Rest a play by George Emlyn Williams.*

The Belisha beacon and zebra markings on the pedestrian crossing suggest that the panorama along Lime Street, showing St George's Hall, dates from the 1950s. Leslie Hore-Belisha, the Minister of Transport in the late 1930s, had the beacons named after him when they were introduced, but the distinctive street markings were not trialled until after the war. The use of the alternating black and white rectangles was not made a requirement in law until 1951. Lime Street was established in 1790, being named after the lime kilns that were in use around here. Doctors at the local infirmary objected to the smells given off by the kilns and had them removed, but the street kept its name. What was something of

an outpost, being beyond the old boundary of the town, became significantly more important to the Liverpudlian way of life in the 1850s. The railway arrived and St George's Hall opened. William Brown Street was set out, linking here with the town centre. The library and museum, the art gallery and a theatre and opera house, the forerunner of the Empire, were all built soon afterwards in the vicinity. Within a very short time, this part of town was a veritable cultural quarter. It was about then that the Waterloo Memorial or Wellington's Column, seen in the distance, was completed. Since 1865, the statue has faced southeast, looking towards the site of his most famous victory across the Channel in central Belgium.

**Above:** Looking north along Strand Street in 1952, we are in the heart of the dockland. With a view across Canning Dock, the main Pier Head buildings of the Harbour Board, Cunard and the Royal Liver are instantly recognisable in the left centre as is the White Star building standing in isolation, to the right. James Street runs away to the right, off towards the city centre. The street after James Street is Red Cross Street – one of the old 'lost streets' of the docks. Elsewhere, in the photograph we can see the remains of the Goree Piazzas and, in the distance the Three Sisters (the chimneys of Clarence Dock power station). In the foreground is the area known as Mann Island that has been redeveloped in recent years to provide waterfront dwelling in large apartment blocks. It is now some six decades since this aerial shot was taken and times have changed. Mann Island was created in the 18th and 19th centuries as part of the dock complex and was itself the site of Manchester Dock, which was filled in just over 75 years ago.

This serene view of the Pier Head was taken in 1962 and shows locals promenading along the front or enjoying the sea breeze as they took time to relax. The face of the Pier Head has altered since then. Prince's and George's Landing Stages that dominated much of the scene were scrapped in 1973 as the trans-Atlantic liner services were discontinued. This once-significant half-mile-long landmark was replaced in 1975 by smaller stages for the local ferry and the one for the Isle of Man crossing. One of these sank in 2006 and had to be replaced the following year.

**Left and bottom left:** This pair of photographs uses St George's Hall as a point of location. In the view taken in the 1950s (bottom left) we are looking away from St. George's Hall pre Churchill Way flyover. In shot to the right is a busy Dale Street car park facing the Mitre pub and Manchester Street is still a thoroughfare. The foundation stone for the Hall was laid in 1838, the year of Queen Victoria's coronation. Building work did not begin until 1842 and it was not until 1854 that it opened for public use. St George's Hall was quite unusual in that it was a multi-purpose building. Initially, the germ of the idea for its construction centred around the provision of a place where triennial music festivals could be held, but as the town also needed a courthouse it was decided to combine the interests. It is almost ironic that you could listen to a classical orchestra performing, dance at a masked ball and watch someone being sentenced to hang, all at the same venue.

> ### *Did you know?*
>
> *The Liverpool Society for the Prevention of Cruelty to Children, the forerunner of the NSPCC, was set up on 19 April, 1883, by Thomas Agnew, a Liverpool banker, with the help of Liverpool MP Samuel Smith.*

**Below:** The raised roadway carrying traffic across equally busy streets below shows just what impact the motorcar was beginning to have upon city life in 1970. Things would not improve because the rapid rise in private motoring that had really taken off in the late 1950s and 1960s was set to become an ever increasing problem as the number of vehicles clogging up urban areas and emitting noxious fumes into the atmosphere seemed to be multiplying at an alarming rate. Two examples of modernist architecture act as a sort of pair of bookmarks in this photograph. On the far right is St John's Beacon, later Radio City Tower, and diners in the revolving restaurant could look across to the building on the left. They would have an excellent view of what is affectionately known as 'Paddy's Wigwam'. This is the Cathedral of Christ the King, the seat of Liverpool's Catholic Archbishop. After the Irish potato famine of the 1840s, there was a significant number of predominantly Catholic migrants from Ireland who settled in Liverpool and the building of a cathedral was planned. However, financial constraints prevented anything more than a Lady Chapel in Everton being completed. Several designs were suggested over the next century and more until, at long last, a modernist design by Francis Gibberd was accepted. The cathedral was built on Hope Street and consecrated in 1967.

# AT WORK

**Right** The public wash house was a boon to the Liverpool housewife. The premises boasted tubs with hot and cold water laid on, hot dryers and pressing machines. To many of the women the wash house became a social gathering; at the same time every week they could meet up with friends and neighbours, have a chat and make new friends. They took the kids, of course, and the children enjoyed the weekly event; they could play with their own friends, get in their mothers' way, and on cold winter days keep warm by sitting snugly on top of one of the dryers. Liverpool has always been a city of firsts, and the city set up the world's first public wash house as far back as 1842.

**Below:** Sugar has been associated with Liverpool for centuries. Henry Tate set up his own refinery in 1862 and expanded this business by moving to the Love Lane site in 1872. The Love Lane Refinery in its time employed

thousands from the surrounding Vauxhall district. In 1921 Tate's amalgamated with Lyle's of Greenock. From there the Tate & Lyle company was formed. Production at the Love Lane factory reached a peak of 550,000 tons in 1972. Despite strong efforts to keep the world famous Tate & Lyle factory in Liverpool open, it closed in 1981, but the name remains, a permanent reminder, above the doors of the art gallery, the Tate Liverpool, on Albert Dock. Henry Tate, himself, was a benefactor on a significant scale – building the Hahnemann Hospital on Hope Street, providing the funds for Liverpool University's library block, as well as generous donations to the Royal Infirmary and Liverpool Institute.

**Below:** There is something very structured and efficient about this 1936 picture from the Vernon's Pools office, in Liverpool. This would have been an ideal job for the all-female workforce in the mid 1930s. It all began In the winter of 1923 when Littlewoods Pools Company was founded, with the first Pools coupons being sold to football fans outside Manchester United's Old Trafford ground. The first ever jackpot, known then as a first dividend, was worth the

princely sum of £2.60. Initially, the business was slow and John Moores bought out his two partners who had lost confidence in the loss-making enterprise. Moores quickly turned Littlewoods round and millions of working people began to spend a few pence each week in what was the only national gambling competition. Vernons Pools was founded in 1925, making Liverpool the centre of an industry that employed thousands of women checking the weekly returns. Playing the Football Pools before the arrival of the internet involved completing by hand the special coupons provided by each of the companies. Initially coupons were readily available from newsagents and tobacconists, places most frequented by the working man. The main football pool companies also provided a service where coupons were hand-delivered directly to players by various networks of collectors across the UK. With the launch of the National Lottery in the UK in 1994, it was feared that the Football Pools would suffer a loss of revenue. However, this has not proven to be the case, as punters have the choice to register their entry online. This photograph, however, is a reminder of the manual contribution from working women to one of the key industries of the city in the twentieth century.

# Griffiths & Armour - Insuring the Right Advice

They had spotted a gap in the market for impartial client-focused advice on insurance. They saw their role as being to analyse the risks their clients ran and to match those risks with the right insurance. If need be they devised new forms of cover, and appropriate policy wordings. The insurance had to fit the client, not the client fit the insurance.

In 1930s Liverpool the market was still marine-insurance dominated. Griffiths & Armour therefore deliberately focused on non-marine risks.

The partners brought intelligence, flair, enterprise and professional qualifications, but above all push, cheek and self-confidence. As young men with no family commitments, they could take a risk. Many in the city today will remember Kenneth Griffiths who died in 1999, and recognise precisely the qualities he must have possessed in his youth.

The firm took its first offices in the Temple in Dale Street right under the noses of their former employers. Kenneth Griffiths' father's firm already had offices in the same building and the address looked impressive on the firm's letterhead. The reality was different. The premises were run-down, and were to become positively squalid in the post war years when modern offices in blitz-torn Liverpool were like gold dust.

The Temple was a rabbit warren. The partners got around the image problem the premises might have caused by visiting clients at their own premises or meeting them for coffee in the lounge of the Exchange Hotel. It was not until 1967 that the firm was able to acquire more modern offices by acting immediately on the rumour of an impending take-over in the insurance market and securing the promise of offices which would be released as a result.

Insurance broker and professional indemnity specialists Griffiths & Armour was formed over 70 years ago. It still trades as a partnership, advising other professional firms on the full spectrum of insurance requirements. Independently-owned, the firm remains free of the shorter-term financial constraints which hamper many competitors.

The Group head office is at 19, Water Street, Liverpool, with further offices in London, Manchester, Glasgow, Dublin and Guernsey.

To succeed in an insurance company in the 1930s Liverpool required long service and a total willingness to conform. Kenneth Griffiths and George Armour were both in their twenties and wanted to do things their way. They resigned their steady, secure jobs and, with a single clerical assistant, put up their plate as Consulting Insurance Brokers.

Since 1987 the firm has occupied freehold premises in Water Street.

George Armour was the son of the Rev H S Green of Sandbach, and nephew and adopted son of Theodore Armour, a noted Rodney Street orthopaedic surgeon. Kenneth Griffiths was a scholar of Merchant Taylors' School

***Above:*** *Kenneth Griffiths, co-founder of the firm.*

some important civil engineering contractor clients. This enabled the firm to survive the war years when new business activity ceased.

Most of the staff were drafted into the services. The partners were left with secretarial assistance only to look after the firm's clients, including their war damage claims. The firm would have disappeared altogether had not all the partners failed the services' medical standards through polio, asthma and diphtheria which was then believed to lead to inevitable heart problems.

and son of Ernest Griffiths a consulting engineer noted for his design of the complex building services in hospitals.

In the year Griffiths & Armour was founded George Armour was elected to the city council as Conservative councillor for Sefton. Within six years he became Chairman of the Passenger Transport Committee: it was under his guidance that the major change from trams to buses took place. He became a JP, an alderman, and was Deputy Leader of the Conservative Group on the council at the time of his death in 1957.

Meanwhile Kenneth Griffiths, generally known as KG, became well-known as a member and later trustee of the Philomathic Society - a local debating society where the city's barristers sharpened their skills - and of other clubs and societies. He rose to senior rank in the Masonic order. Nationally, he raised the firm's profile within the insurance world through his vigorous involvement in the affairs of the Chartered Insurance Institute. Even in its early years his reputation gained the firm a level of recognition quite out of proportion to its size.

The partners persuaded a number of well-known names in inter-war Liverpool to entrust their insurance to the new firm: names such as Philip Son & Nephew who not only sold books but also produced the school atlas many of us learnt geography from, Chadburns, then a famous manufacturer of marine telegraph equipment and expanding into other engineering activities, and Collinsons Cut Soles, now lost to the inroads of synthetic materials into the market for leather soles.

A third partner, James Allen, eventually joined the firm. James Allen was in his early forties and brought with him

***Above and below:*** *Views of Dale Street, former home of the firm.*

Happily, all the staff returned from the war and a new wave of expansion began.

The last days of the war saw Griffiths & Armour win an appointment which was to shape the whole future of the firm. It was obvious that following the devastation of the war years that there would have to be a major effort to rebuild what German bombs had destroyed. The design professions were gearing themselves up for that effort and the question of professional liability came up. KG's family connection with consulting engineering led to an interview with the secretary and committee of 'ACE', the Association of Consulting Engineers, in competition with London brokers. Griffiths & Armour's ideas prevailed. But in those days the risk was light - as it remained for another 20 years - and the income from professional indemnity insurance was minimal. The firm remained, as it had always been, a general insurance broker serving a range of industrial, commercial and construction clients.

The initial importance of the connection with ACE was not on the liability side but its introduction to a range of small, but rapidly growing, firms which needed good pension funds. The partners built up a substantial block of pension business based on the then innovative deposit administration model which linked the investment return on a pension fund to the insurers' own investment performance - in effect an early prototype of unit-linking still popular in many investment products.

Sadly, George Armour died, whilst still in his forties, in 1957. KG was approaching his fifties and James Allen was already over 60. Having always been characters they had allowed their idiosyncrasies full rein. KG was a night owl. He appeared in the office around mid-day, left for lunch and a game of bridge in the Constitutional Club and returned to begin his real working day at around tea-time. His staff were expected to stay on in the office until he chose to go home. He then read 'the pinks', flimsy pink-paper carbon copies of every letter that had left the office that day. His scrutiny certainly enforced high quality, both of technical content and of English grammar, but it was symptomatic of an almost paranoid need to control all that went on in the firm. There was little scope for initiative on the part of others. Indeed he regarded 'selling' as a dirty word. Griffiths & Armour waited to be asked to advise. Except of course for KG himself! He would sell the firm's services, as opposed to selling insurance, on every possible occasion and with an unparalleled persistence. Perhaps the firm won many accounts merely because the potential client found that was the only possible way of escape. Maybe they were happily surprised to find that

*Right:* Water Street, now home to Griffiths & Armour, pictured in 1952.

Griffiths & Armour really did deliver the quality of advice and service which KG promised. Many of those people and their business are still clients of Griffiths & Armour today.

Meanwhile, James Allen had more or less retired from the office for health reasons. The air in Liverpool was very seldom clean enough to permit him to come into town at all. Instead he conducted business from his permanent lunch table at the Prince of Wales Hotel in Southport where his clients had regular meetings with him. He must have had great magic, as well as his considerable charm, to persuade them that his services were worth the enormous amount of time these meetings absorbed. The 1950s and 60s, however, were a more leisured age. The entire firm took morning coffee and afternoon tea in Fuller's, along with many others of the insurance fraternity. Perhaps, with a little more enterprise Fuller's of Liverpool could have rivalled Lloyds of London. Sadly, it succumbed to the increasing pace of business life and to the automatic coffee-making machine.

Growth continued but there was no long-term planning, and no will on the part of the founders to allow control to go out of their families. Change only began with the introduction of Brian and Mark Griffiths as partners in the late 1960s, and with a new non-family partner, Derek Pownall, in the early 1970s.

Griffiths & Armour of the 1960s and the Griffiths & Armour which emerged in the 1980s were vastly different.

The firm's business mix was changing dramatically. The clients brought in by James Allen and George Armour were being eroded by take-overs and not replaced with similar commercial and industrial accounts because there were no partners dedicated to that side of the firm's business. On the other hand the firm's professional client base was expanding: the potential liabilities those clients faced were growing exponentially, and their insurance needs growing to match. The financial services side, acting mainly for the same clients, was also expanding. These divisions of the business were absorbing trained staff as rapidly as they could be developed.

By the end of the 1970s the partnership had expanded, and the younger generation was in practical control. Mark Griffiths succeeded his father formally as senior partner in 1984. The first task was to secure what the firm already had in an increasingly competitive environment. That involved moving up a gear from a focus on insurance, but with a strong emphasis on service and claims handling as well simply arranging cover. For the firm's construction clients that involved not only a focus on internal risk reduction, but equally a major involvement in monitoring and influencing legislative change, the development of industry standard contracts, and in lobbying for change in construction procurement methods.

Griffiths & Armour now contributed regularly to responses to government white papers, and advised not only the Association of Consulting Engineers but many other construction institutions, the British Consultants Bureau, the Construction Industry Council, the European Federation of Engineering Consultancy Associations and the International Federation of Consulting Engineers. As long ago as 1972 the firm was asked to help establish a professional indemnity insurance scheme for the South African Association of Consulting Engineers and it began arranging schemes in Ireland, Hong Kong and Turkey. The firm also began working on expanding its insurance service to the legal profession.

The firm continued to build its financial services wing as a separate company in the

*Top: George Armour. **Left:** A silver plate presented to Kenneth Griffiths in 1997 in recognition for outstanding service to The Chartered Insurance Institute.*

group, Griffiths & Armour Financial Services. It also rebuilt and expanded its commercial and industrial account to become the first choice broker for north-western businesses.

Most other major brokers are either quoted on the Stock Exchange, or owned by organisations whose philosophy is to retain their investment only for a relatively short time and for a quick profit. Griffiths & Armour by contrast remains wholly owned by current and former partners. As such it has no need to satisfy the short term requirements of stock market analysts. Its focus is on its service to clients. That is as attractive to people who wish to give a first-class service as it is to clients who seek that standard of service.

In 2003 a number of older partners retired and the management of the firm passed to a younger generation.

This led to a review of the business. Non-core operations – including most of the London and Financial Services businesses - were sold off and overseas operations closed.

Following that exercise the firm re-focussed on specialising in insurance broking, claims and risk management.

In 2010 the firm was appointed as UK partner in a worldwide network of independent insurance brokers - Assurex. Membership of Assurex provides Griffiths & Armour with a truly global reach, and enables the firm to win new clients who trade internationally.

The creation of two egocentric and opinionated young men in the 1930s has come a long way. And if the commitment of present and future partners and staff matches that of their predecessors, then Griffiths & Armour has an equally long run ahead of it as a standard bearer for Merseyside.

*Below: Drury House, home of the firm today.*

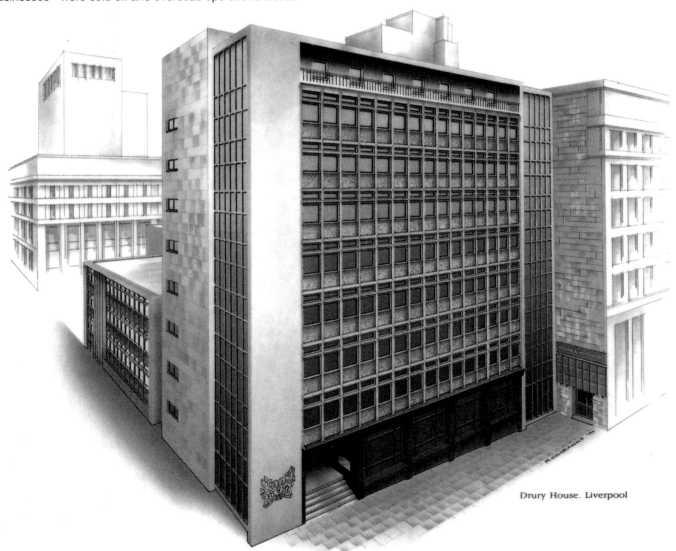

Drury House. Liverpool

# John Mason International
## A Firm on the Move

Among the most familiar sights around Liverpool are the yellow-liveried vans of the removal firm of John Mason International Ltd. And if you aren't old enough to recall removals being made by horse-drawn vehicles there were certainly many members of the Mason family whose memories went so far back.

It was in 1884 that the firm was founded by Mrs Mary Mason in Wavertree, a township then on the outskirts of Liverpool. Before starting out on her own Mary Mason had earlier helped her husband John in his carting business. When Mary's son, also John, began helping her in 1887 coal deliveries became the main activity. In 1890, Mary's 17-year-old son took over and expanded the business into general carrying. In that same year a contract was signed with a local company that was to last for 68 years.

Young John Mason had seen the need for a general carrying service and though at first he had only a pony and cart he expanded the small business by offering to carry anything anywhere. The firm's early records show that a wide variety of goods were carried including laundry to and from the large houses of the wealthy merchants who then lived in the residential districts of Wavertree and Woolton. One of those early contracts was to carry laundry for the Liverpool School for the Blind between its Wavertree and Liverpool establishments - a contract that would be held until 1958 when the city establishment was closed.

*Top:* John Mason with one of his first horse and carts. *Left: Mrs Mary Mason outside her home in 85 High Street, Wavertree, 1900. The office was run from this house.*

and selling them for himself and for others. His judgement was so respected that he bought and sold horses for a number of the principal dock contractors, and even Lord Sefton entrusted him with commissions to buy horses on his behalf. John would regularly spend a day each month at the Craven Arms Horse Repository; he was also keen on entering his horses in agricultural shows where his horses won many prizes.

By 1914 and the outbreak of the First World War John Mason had built up a thriving firm engaged in coal retailing, general haulage and household removals. Although the shortage of horses during the war would restrict business John's astuteness ensured that the

John Mason married Mary Hannah Baker in 1897 and from then on she assisted her husband with the clerical and book keeping work she would later continue to do for her sons in their turn.

Before long more vehicles and heavier horses were acquired. Furniture vans were built to John Mason's requirements. From the small firm's base at 85 High Street, the Mason family home, the first long distance removals were undertaken in 1900 using horse-drawn vehicles. Early customers included the Anglo American Oil Company, which would become Esso, the Cheshire Lines Railway Company and the English Margarine Works.

In 1904, when work started on the Liverpool Anglican Cathedral, the aptly named John Mason carried much of the carved stonework for Morrisons Ltd, the firm given the contract to build the Cathedral.

The firm's activities soon extended not only to Liverpool but to Manchester, many parts of Lancashire, Cheshire and North Wales using horse-drawn vehicles, whilst longer distances, those over 50 miles, were covered by rail.

business did not falter. In 1917 the business moved to 127, High Street, Wavertree, gaining more space for warehousing and stabling for the firm's horses.

Leslie Mason, John and Mary's eldest son born in 1904, entered the business in his early teens; he would play a full part in the firm for almost fifty years. Leslie had shown an early interest from childhood and at the age of only 12 was already helping by driving a pony and wagon like his father before him. By the age of 16 Leslie

Liverpool was growing, and as new districts were being developed contracts were obtained from the City Corporation to carry material to and from the new roads being constructed. John Mason was a man of great energy and enterprise and never afraid of hard work - if necessary doing so round the clock.

John Mason had a great passion for horses: his only hobby was buying

*Top left: John Mason driving one of his first horse-drawn vans. A similar vehicle has been lent to Liverpool Transport Museum.* **Left:** *127 High Street - the second family home and office since the early 1920s.* **Above:** *One of the first motor vehicles to be purchased - French manufactured Aries.*

was driving a team of horses, helping to overcome the wartime manpower shortage and enabling him to learn the business from a practical point of view.

When the firm's first motor vehicle, an Albion, was acquired in 1921 it had solid tyres and a chain drive. Although more motor vehicles would be steadily added to the fleet, horse transport would still be the main form of transport for some time, and horses continued to be bought for many years. It would not be until almost the outbreak of the Second World War that all horse-drawn vehicles would be replaced by motor vans, platform vehicles and lift vans.

In the meantime, with the increasing help of Leslie Mason, the business developed. Its reputation for good workmanship and the personal attention and courtesy of its employees became ever more widely known.

The first lift vans for rail were bought in 1926 and overseas agents were appointed to look after the firm's interests abroad. A year before the outbreak of the second world war in 1938 John Mason's second son Stanley joined the business. Born in 1921, Stanley would play a major role in developing the company, but

his practical training involving driving and packing was interrupted in 1941 by being called up to serve in the Merchant Navy for the duration of the war.

Just as in the First World War domestic moves were much reduced, though contracts gained from the government helped keep the business going despite both a manpower shortage and petrol rationing. The Second World War, which brought to an end the era of the horse-drawn vehicle, saw the firm's motorised vehicles being called up for war service. One of the many interesting jobs undertaken was the continuous removal of the Royal Liverpool Philharmonic Orchestra's instruments around the country enabling it to continue to give regular performances. The orchestra gave many concerts to troops and civilians during the war years. Mason's driver, Bill Clarke, was never late for a concert even though he had to contend with all the hazards of the blackout and enemy bombing.

In the war years Masons did vital work evacuating schools, institutions, government departments, commercial and industrial concerns and homes. Munitions and other war equipment were carried, whilst to meet the call for decentralisation extra warehouses were acquired on the outskirts of the city and at Penmaenmawr, in North Wales, for furniture storage. Each evening during the intense bombing of Liverpool the Mason team played its part with Mason vehicles reporting for duty at Civil Defence and Fire Posts.

*Top:* One of the first Albion's, purchased c1921. **Left:** *Mason's first pneumatic tyred vehicle. A forerunner of the modern fleet.* **Above:** *A vehicle permanently engaged in moving the musical instruments of the Philharmonic Orchestra around the country during the Second World War.*

distribution in the London area and return loading. In 1950, the company became one of the founder members of FIDI - the world-wide Federation of International Furniture Removers.

John Mason, who had retired at the end of the war, died in 1953. Leslie and Stanley had become joint managing directors. In 1948 the business had grown to such an extent that the private limited company of John Mason (Wavertree) Ltd had been formed with John and Mary Mason, with sons Leslie and Stanley, as its directors.

*Above: The drive-on drive-off service from Preston to Larne, Mason's were one of the first companies to use this service. Above left: The fleet pictured in front of Liverpool Cathedral during the 1960s. Below: A horse-drawn van being exhibited at Liverpool Show during the 1950s.*

The war's end brought with it the enormous problems of rebuilding after the destruction of the blitz. Industry and commerce had to be reorganised to meet the needs of the post-war world. The Mason brothers, with hard work and foresight, made great progress. Large office removals were undertaken and a considerable contribution made to the transport services required by the vast rebuilding programme which would take place.

In some cases weeks of pre-planning were necessary for the removals of private and government offices to ensure the minimum disruption of office routine, and several had to be undertaken at weekends. Hundreds of tons of files, papers and office equipment were involved in one of the largest moves in which the Inland Revenue, Ministry of Food and other Ministerial offices were transferred from Llandudno to London.

A daily removal service from Liverpool to London was started in 1948; London depot facilities would be eventually acquired from FL Pettman Ltd to facilitate

To ensure reliability all vehicles had always to be kept in first class condition so that delivery promises could be honoured. Now the fleet and equipment would be kept constantly up to date by the purchase of new vehicles. Steady expansion of Mason's service was made to cover the whole of the United Kingdom.

A daily removal service to Ireland using the Preston/Larne roll-on roll-off ferry began in 1955. Combined with the daily Liverpool/London service this offered the fastest route available from the capital to Ireland. Mason's would be one of the first removal firms to use the ferry service from Preston, and at the time be the only firm in the north west offering an almost daily service to Ireland of articulated trailer vans, a service offering considerable

savings in packing and handling costs since loading on and off the ferry by cranes was no longer needed.

To help provide a more local service in Cheshire in 1955 Leslie and Stanley became directors of B Dudley & Sons Ltd - Removers of Bebington, a firm established in 1869. Both companies worked in close association. In 1959 Dudley's would be taken over completely by Masons.
By the end of the 1950s Masons, in association with four reputable South of England firms, had also established a network of distribution routes serving the Midlands, the South West, the South East and the South of England as well as many parts of Wales, Lancashire and Yorkshire.

A new 16,000 sq. ft warehouse was opened in Wavertree in 1959, built to the company's specifications and specially designed and constructed to store customers' effects with the highest possible degree of safety. By 1962 the continued growth of the company resulted in the purchase of a 36,000 sq. ft warehouse in Kirby.

The company now launched into the antique shipping business, which required large consolidation and storage facilities. By 1967 a further 2,000 sq. ft warehouse was acquired bringing the company's total Merseyside facilities to 72,000 sq ft.

*Above: Mason's won first prize in an FIDI photography competition in the section entitled "A Most Beautiful Removal". Below: A Mason's van and trailer pictured in front of the Liver Building, 1958.*

Stanley Mason was elected President of the Overseas Division of the British Association of Removers in 1965. Six years later, 1971 began sadly with Leslie Mason's death, following which Stanley's wife, Jean, joined her husband as a director. Their eldest son Paul joined the business in 1972.

In 1974 the company joined Eurovan, a consortium of around 180 mainly privately-owned world wide removal companies, and by 1977 a record volume of antique shipping was recorded - some 250 ISO containers were packed and despatched from the company's warehouses. By 1982 that success was consolidated with a record year for inter-continental removals: over 400 containers were exported winning the company the Eurovan 'Biggest Booker' award.

Stanley Mason died the following year, in April 1983; his son Paul now joined his mother Jean as a director of the company.

More than a century of successful trading had been achieved, not only through the hard work of the directors but very much because the company had always enjoyed a loyal and hard working staff. Their contribution above all else has played the central role in the growth and development of the business. It was in that spirit that in 1984 the firm entered its second century.

In 1989 all the company's local activities were transferred to 35, Wilson Road, Huyton, whilst a new warehouse and offices were opened in Croydon.

Sadly, Paul Mason passed away in 2009. His wife Vivien then became a Director. The fifth generation of the family, Caroline and Simon Mason, joined the business in the same year. Caroline graduated from the University of Leeds with a degree in Business Management and Spanish and Simon from the University of Manchester, achieving a First Class degree in International Business. Since joining the company, both Caroline and Simon have embarked on an extensive training programme within the industry: Simon completed most of his training in the USA to gain experience from an international perspective, and Caroline learned about the business in both Liverpool and London.

Today, international, commercial and household moves and storage are at the core of the firm's business. Mason's currently facilitates over 8,000 removals each year across the globe. From a single horse and cart and undertaking only local work, the firm of John Mason International Ltd has grown into a major player on the world stage. But despite its massive growth the firm has managed to retain the virtues of a small family firm: flexibility, a genuine appreciation of its employees and an unswerving commitment to meeting its clients' needs.

*Top left:* Delivering a grand piano to the QEII. *Above left:* John Mason's International House, Huyton Business Park, premises. *Above right:* Simon and Caroline Mason.

# Liverpool Hope University
## A University with a Difference

Liverpool Hope University is unlike any other university in the United Kingdom. Its work has been shaped for over 165 years by Christian principles, but it embraces those of all faiths and of none. Today several thousand students, both undergraduate and post-graduate study at the University.

The University prides itself on the quality of its teaching, learning and scholarship. It seeks the highest academic standards whilst helping students to become responsible citizens of the world. True to the collegial tradition, it values the individual, with care, concern and support for students always a priority.

Liverpool Hope is an ecumenical Christian Foundation which strives to provide opportunities for the well-rounded personal development of Christians and students from other faiths and beliefs, educating the whole person in mind, body and spirit, irrespective of age, social or ethnic origins or physical capacity, including in particular those who might otherwise not have had an opportunity to enter higher education. The University is a national provider of a wide range of high quality programmes responsive to the needs of students, including the education, training and professional development of teachers for Church and state schools.

It aims to sustain an academic community, as a sign of hope, enriched by Christian values and worship, which supports teaching and learning, scholarship and research, encourages the understanding of Christian and other faiths and beliefs and promotes religious and social harmony.

Hope's mission statement includes the objective 'To contribute to the educational, religious, cultural, social and economic life of Liverpool, Merseyside, the North-West and beyond', reflecting the faith values of the University's name and origins. As the only ecumenical Christian HE institution in Europe, the University commemorates its foundation

annually and holds a weekly Foundation Hour when all other activities give way to an opportunity to reflect on the University's values. The setting aside of the Foundation Hour as a protected period reflects the University's commitment to its founding and continuing values.

**Top:** *Liverpool Hope University's coat of arms.* **Left and above:** *Early views of Notre Dame training college, where it all began.*

men were noted for their work in healing sectarian divisions within Liverpool during the 1970s and 80s. In addition, they shared the ambition for an ecumenical foundation in Liverpool Hope.

On arrival in Liverpool in 1976 as its new Roman Catholic Archbishop Derek Worlock's first visitor was the city's Anglican Bishop, David Sheppard, former England opening bat and an old friend, who came bearing a bottle of wine. They became inseparable, and were known as Tweedledum and Tweedledee - or, in the Scouse vernacular (because they were always seen together in the newspaper) 'Fish 'n' Chips'. They stood in for each other and sometimes preached joint sermons in which one would complete the thought of the other. Their principle was 'Do everything together, except the things

Staff believe the quality of the educational experience at Liverpool Hope University matches the best available. They do not believe that education is just about equipping people for the world of work; they also educate students for the work of the world.

We live in a time of change – social, political and economic. The University believes that only students educated within a global context can constructively, fairly and bravely make the changes the world needs.

which conscience forces us to do apart'. In a Liverpool, which had the potential to be a English Belfast, and in which older people could remember rowdy Orange marches, this

Liverpool Hope University has two campuses, one three miles from the city centre, the other within a brisk walk of it. Students based at both Hope Park and The Creative Campus will find relaxed and inspiring places in which to learn. There is also an outdoor centre at Plas Caerdeon in Wales.

*Top left: The 1933/34 netball team.* **Above:** *Bishop David Sheppard and Archbishop Derek Worlock.* **Below and inset:** *Then and now; sudy bedrooms from the 1960s and 2011.*

The landscaped green spaces of Hope Park provide a tranquil environment for academic study and debate. Scholars and students can relax and mingle away from the bustle of the city centre, enjoying a library with extended opening hours.

The Sheppard-Worlock Library is the University's central library, based at the Hope Park campus. Housed alongside the Hilda Constance Allen Building, the library offers extended hours throughout the year, including periods of 24 hour opening at exam times.

The Library takes its name from Bishop David Sheppard and Archbishop Derek Worlock. The two

was as dramatic as it was novel.

They stood together in all the problems and crises of Liverpool: the Heysel stadium disaster; unemployment; the Toxteth riots; housing and civic scandals and the IRA bombs in Warrington. But it was not just a cosy Catholic-Anglican club. The Church Leaders Group also included Dr John Newton, Methodist superintendent, John Williamson of the United Reformed Church, the Baptist Trevor Hubbard and Col. Lily Farrar of the Salvation Army. Together they found a distinctive Merseyside voice in addressing the social problems of the Thatcher era, of whose individualist ethos they were sharply critical. In Liverpool they kept alive forgotten notions such as common good and community. They refused to believe that the weakest or the unemployed should go to the wall.

On an historic visit to London, Archbishop Derek Worlock and Bishop David Sheppard secured from the Secretary of State for Education permission to create an ecumenical institute of higher education. The story goes that the Secretary of State, Gordon Oaks (who was MP for the nearby constituency of Widnes) was not particularly concerned about the constitution of the new institute as he believed it would not last a year!

In 1997, one of the final acts of Dr. Jim Burke as Rector was to approve the building of a new library at a cost of £5.34million – the Sheppard-Worlock library.

In addition to a wealth of publications, research material and extensive computing facilities the library also plays host to a number of commercial activities in the business and education communities. The library houses a number of research collections. These include the Gradwell Collection: This collection, entrusted to Liverpool Hope on the closure of St. Joseph's College at Upholland, contains material covering theology, philosophy, church, secular and local history, ecclesiastical history, art, architecture, sociology, education and works of general reference. It also includes recusant works and early printed works.

**Top left:** *Notre Dame library circa 1900.* **Above:** *Studying in the library in the 1960s.* **Left:** *The Gradwell Library.*

The Picton Collection is a collection of theology material on long-term loan from the Liverpool City Library. This collection contains many of the classic New Testament works published before 1975, some old but extremely useful linguistic studies including older Hebrew, Aramaic and Greek lexicons, and several sets of theological texts. The Gradwell and Picton collections not only enhance but complement The Sheppard-Worlock's own collection of theology holdings, both lending and reference.

Hope has been fortunate enough to receive materials from the estate of Archbishop Stuart Blanch (1918–1994).The collection includes notes from his student days at Wycliffe Hall, Oxford and notes for sermons, lectures, talks and speeches made while Bishop of Liverpool (1960–1966) and Archbishop of York (1975–1983).

Materials have been donated to create a library for the Centre for the Study of African Asian Christianity by

Professor Andrew F. Walls, University of Edinburgh (Centre for the Study of Christianity in the Non-Western World) and the University of Aberdeen. The Library offers resources across a range of mission studies, its principal focus being Africa and the Asia-Pacific region.

Books, pamphlets and journals on education and related subjects donated by the University of Liverpool form the Education Research Collection. The collection contains 30,000 books and pamphlets. These include books on all aspects of education, particularly from an historic viewpoint and with large sections on special education and religious education. There are also collections of bibliographies, Government publications, Government and other statistical publications, and annual reports of organisations connected with education; 400 journals,

*Top right:* Former S.Katharine's Chapel, now the Senate Room. *Left:* A Notre Dame reunion in Hope Chapel 2010. *Below and inset:* Hilda Constance Allen (inset) and the building named in her honour.

Meanwhile massive investment of over £20m has been made on new buildings in the past few years. The Creative Campus has two main buildings and gardens modelled on those of renaissance Italy. The Cornerstone is based in the former St Francis Xavier School, an imposing example of 19th century architecture transformed by an award-winning and sensitive restoration into a 21st century centre for learning.

September 2010 saw the launch of the new £8.5m Eden (Education and Enterprise) Centre, with 20 new classrooms and new learning and social areas, as well as international conference facilities and business incubation space. Earlier in 2010, the £4.3 million Capstone building opened at The Creative Campus, housing the University's Centre for Music Performance and Innovation, as well as the spectacular Hope Theatre with its perfect acoustic environment.

*Left:* HM The Queen and The Duke of Edinburgh's visit to The Cornerstone 2004. **Bottom:** Angel Field and Capstone Theatre, 2010. **Below:** The Capstone Theatre concert band.

with strengths in learning difficulties and special education, educational psychology, and education overseas.

The Centre for Millennialism Studies is focused on the study of contemporary manifestations of millennialism/apocalypticism; particularly the 'afterlife' of apocalyptic texts and ideas within popular culture.

Global Hope charity. In 2010, 11 Global Hope projects took place in seven countries on three continents.

There has been a large growth in student numbers in the last decade. By 2011 there were over 8000 students. A key feature of the University is the Network of Hope, an outreach programme to higher education (HE) 'cold spots' in Lancashire through Holy Cross, Bury and St. Mary's, Blackburn Roman Catholic sixth form colleges. Over 600 FTE students study Liverpool Hope programmes through the Network of Hope.

As thousands of students have discovered for themselves the University's motto 'In Faith, Hope and Love' are not simply words.

The University originated in three teaching training colleges. The Warrington Training College (later named S.Katharine's) was founded in 1844 by the Church of England, and Notre Dame College by the Roman Catholic Sisters of Notre Dame in 1856, to promote mass education through the training of women teachers. In 1964 the Catholic Education Council established Christ's College as a teacher training college for men and women. The institutions diversified their curricula during the 1970s and a federal ecumenical body, the Liverpool Institute of Higher Education, was founded in 1980 and located on a single site, Hope Park, in the Childwall area of the city. A further campus has subsequently been developed at Everton and there is also an outdoor education and residential study centre in North Wales. The name Liverpool Hope was adopted in 1995 and the institution became Liverpool Hope University College in 2002, following the grant of taught degree awarding powers. University status was granted by a decision of the Privy Council in spring 2005 followed by acceptance by the Privy Council of the institution's suggested renaming as Liverpool Hope University.

In September 2009 Liverpool Hope was granted Research Degree Awarding Powers (RDAP) making it a fully-fledged University.

Hope is a community where each student is known by name, and not just as a number. The student body is drawn from dozens of countries, including the United States, Nigeria, China and Bangladesh. Students are given the chance to study abroad, as well as undertaking overseas work as part of the Service and Leadership Award, via the University's

*Above left:* Liverpool Hope University's girls hockey team ready for action. ***Below:*** Inside the Education Building in 2010.

# Eli Lilly - The Answer That Matters

One of the region's most important and respected enterprises is Eli Lilly and Company Ltd's bulk manufacturing facility in Fleming Road, Speke. Lilly's mission is to provide customers with 'Answers that Matter' through innovative medicines, information, and exceptional customer service, that enable people to live longer, healthier and more active lives. And as the Speke mission and product mix changes to become focused on animal healthcare, that mission extends, providing trusted solutions through products for both farmed and companion animals.

Not only has the local economy benefited enormously from the presence of the plant, but those who have worked there can also look back with pride at being involved in an enterprise which has helped millions of people.

UK operations began in 1934 when Lilly established a small sales office in central London. The company opened its first manufacturing facility outside the US in Basingstoke in 1939, the day after war was declared.

The story of Eli Lilly and Company goes back to 1876 when Colonel Eli Lilly opened a small pharmaceutical business in Indianapolis in the USA.

At the age of 38 Eli Lilly had not had a happy life: he had been captured and become a prisoner during the American Civil War. During his captivity his wife had died in childbirth. On his release Eli tried his hand at being a cotton planter but went bankrupt. He put the last of his savings into another type of business entirely.

Seldom has $1,400 been better invested. Eli began with two employees and a month later would take on a third - his fourteen year old son, and eventual successor, Josiah Kirby Lilly.

Eli Lilly and Company was unorthodox from the start – its purpose was to specialise in 'ethical' drugs to be dispensed at the suggestion of enlightened physicians rather than in response to the eloquence of medicine-show hucksters – the latter being very common at the time. The Colonel vowed that his medicines would be based on the best science of the day, and quality was paramount. Eli Lilly said to his son, "take what you find here and make it better and better. No business worthwhile can be built upon anything but the best in everything." That ethic continues to this day.

Sales in the first year of business averaged less than $1,000 a month. A century later Eli Lilly and Company would have more than 23,000 employees and annual sales worldwide of more than a billion dollars.

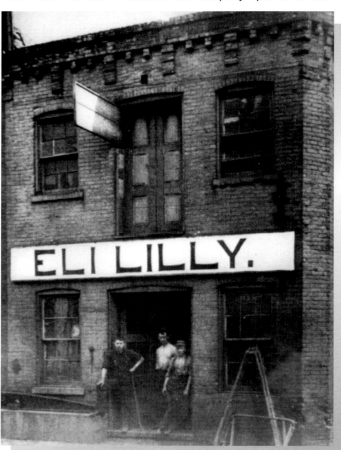

*Top: Colonel Eli Lilly. **Above right:** Josiah K Lilly Sr, son of the founder. **Left:** Where it all began, Eli Lilly's small pharmaceutical company in Indianapolis, USA.*

By 1898 when Colonel Eli died, the firm was selling over 2,000 products.

But it was to be insulin which propelled the company to the forefront of the pharmaceutical industry. In 1921 Frederick G Banting and Charles H Best made one of the greatest breakthroughs in medicine - they discovered insulin, the first substance found to help control diabetes. In May, 1922, Eli Lilly staff were invited by the University of Toronto to help in developing a process for refining insulin and its manufacture. By August Lilly scientists had worked out improved methods for the purification and large-scale production. By the end of 1923 insulin would become available to millions.

Meanwhile, in Britain, another important story was unfolding.

One of the most famous names in history is that of Alexander Fleming (1881-1955) and his discovery of penicillin.

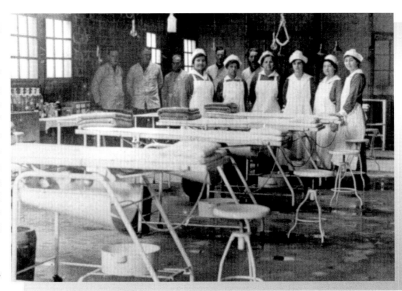

However, though Fleming found that the extract 'penicillin' would attack a range of bacteria, he initially concluded that it was useless for treating the sick. The glory of the penicillin story passed to two other men: Howard Florey and Ernst Chain.

An Australian, Howard Walter Florey (1898-1968), was a Professor of Pathology in Oxford. In the mid-1930s Florey invited a German-Jewish colleague anxious to quit Hitler's Germany, biochemist Ernst Boris Chain (1906-1979), to join his research team.

*Top: A medical field hospital in Contrexeville, France, set up in 1917 during the first world war by Lilly in partnership with the American Red Cross. Left: Lilly was among the first pharmaceutical companies to mass-produce penicillin. Below: A view inside the laboratory in 1946.*

Every schoolchild can recall the tale of how in August, 1928, Fleming was in his laboratory and about to wash out an old petri dish on which he had been cultivating some staphylococcus bacteria. Suddenly he noticed that a strange mould which had begun growing in the bottom of the dish was killing the bacteria.

The mould turned out to be penicillium; Fleming's chance observation would lead to fame, fortune and a knighthood - and save the lives of millions.

Fleming gave the language a new word 'penicillin' which he coined in a paper published in 1929, using the word as shorthand for the 'mould broth filtrate' which he had extracted from the penicillium whilst trying to distil its active ingredient.

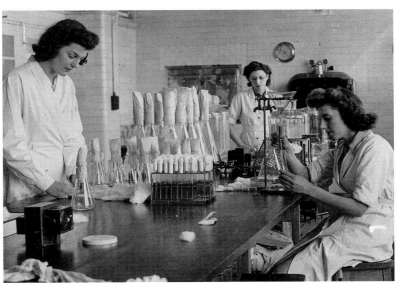

In the late 1930s Florey and Chain picked up the ball, which had been dropped by Fleming. Together the pair devised improved techniques for manufacturing and purifying penicillin before embarking on an extensive series of trials and experiments.

In 1940 the first human recipient of penicillin was an Oxford policeman with blood poisoning; he began to recover, then tragically relapsed and died because not enough penicillin was available to continue the treatment. The next recipient however, was a boy with coxitis who recovered.

Initially the quantities of penicillin being produced were tiny. True industrial production only arrived with American involvement in the Second World War. The vast resources of the USA were harnessed to produce penicillin in huge quantities, with Allied casualties in Tunisia and Sicily in 1943 being the first to benefit from the new antibiotic.

Fleming and Florey were knighted in 1944. In 1945 Fleming, Florey and Chain jointly received the Nobel Prize.

Meanwhile the Ministry of Supply had been looking into the possibility of building a penicillin plant in Britain to match those being built in the USA. The top secret wartime project was known as Job 800.

In 1944, soon after the D-day landings in Europe, a fermentation plant was built at Speke operated by the Distillers Company on behalf of the Ministry of Supply. The new plant was built on a green field site marked by two enormous bomb craters, reminders of the Luftwaffe's blitz.

Distillers already had three other plants in the area from where it could draw a skeleton staff of process workers, supervisors and engineers. And there were good supplies of water nearby – critical for use in the fermentation process.

The Speke plant was an almost exact copy of a penicillin plant in Terre Haute, Indiana, in the USA. Batch 0001 was ready for sale by the end of December. Soon every doctor in Britain was able to prescribe the previously rare and much sought after medicine.

In 1946 the road on which the plant stood was renamed Fleming Road. Two years later Sir Alexander Fleming himself visited the site and was moved to tears by what he saw.

Fleming died in 1955. That year, the tenth anniversary of the first production at Speke, a Fleming memorial was unveiled on the site.

**Top:** *Third and fourth generations of Lilly, Eli Lilly and Josiah K Lilly, Jr.* **Above:** *Aerial view of the site in the 1950s.* **Left:** *At work in the Fermenter House in 1954.*

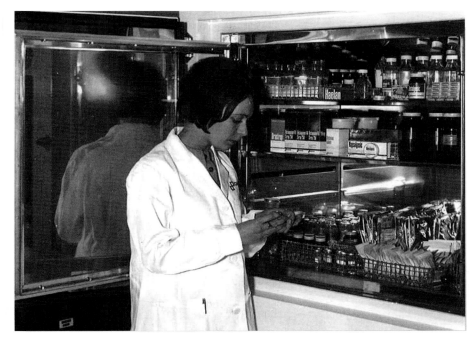

name would plant the company's name firmly in the public consciousness.

Major upgrades to the plant took place in 1970. Work began on a fourth fermenting house, whilst the old No 1 fermenting house was dismantled and penicillin production on the site ended. There would only be two large fermenting houses left on site - confusingly to the uninitiated named Nos 3 and 4. In 1980 came an £8.5 million investment in four 30,000 gallon (150,000 litre) fermentation tanks, which were inspected by the Duke of Gloucester on a Royal visit to the plant the following year.

Further expansion would involve the production of biosynthetic insulin.

In 1979, the 50th anniversary of Fleming's paper on penicillin, Lilly Speke celebrated with a special lunch. The highlight was the starter 'Pate a la Petrie' a brown jelly representing the culture medium, a white surface representing the colony of staphylococci and a green mould for the penicillium - an edible reminder of Fleming's remarkable discovery.

The Speke plant worked closely with Eli Lilly and Company in Indianapolis, and by the early 1950s started work on one of its new antibiotics - erythromycin. This was another top-secret project. Erythromycin was referred to as Product 322 after the lock number of the building in which it was fermented - the No 3 Fermenter House.

Eli Lilly and Company acquired the Speke plant from Distillers in 1962 and a new name was introduced on 1st January, 1963. For the next three decades the plant would trade under the name of Dista Products rather than under that of Eli Lilly. Lilly had thought of calling the business the Kirby Manufacturing Company after the traditional second name of the Lilly family's sons, though in the end Dista prevailed, taking its name from Distaquaine, an important pharmaceutical product.

The Speke plant began to concentrate on the fermentation of a new Lilly product 'Tylosin' the world's first antibiotic created exclusively for animal use. The first batch was produced at Speke in August, 1963: the next year saw five more Tylosin formulations being fermented at Speke.

The biggest boost to Speke in this period however, came early in 1964. The Dista marketing division came up with the name Distalgesic for Dista's new analgesic or painkiller - the

In 1922 in the USA Lilly had became the first pharmaceutical company in the world to produce insulin on an industrial

*Above:* Stability laboratories in 1968, where samples of products already released to the market are retained for that product's shelf life *Below:* Eli Lilly's Packing Line in 1966.

embarked on a public-private partnership to increase the number of trained personnel, the quantity of drugs available and the transfer of technological know-how to countries where the disease was most prevalent.

A public-private initiative, the Lilly MDR-TB Partnership encompasses global health and relief organisations, academic institutions and private companies. Its mission is to address the expanding crisis of MDR-TB. The Partnership mobilises more than 20 healthcare partners on five continents. Lilly has contributed £70m in cash, medicines,

scale. The insulin was extracted from the pancreatic glands of animals. In 1980, for the first time in history, a diabetic received with insulin produced synthetically - using DNA technology or 'genetic engineering' - which unlike animal-sourced insulin, was identical to that found in the human body. Dista Products took a key role in fermenting material used for development, clinical work and sales. In April, 1982, Dista's £5 million biosynthetic human insulin plant was officially opened by then Secretary of State for the Environment, the Rt. Hon Michael Heseltine.

Lilly Speke now manufactures the entire world supply for the Lilly market of a biosynthetic human growth hormone manufactured using recombinant DNA technology – and become the largest bulk biotechnology manufacturing company in the UK – a position consolidated by the construction of a £50 million state-of-the-art manufacturing facility to make human growth hormone.

Meanwhile, something which the site had manufactured for several decades in small quantities Capreomycin – an antibiotic used to treat Multi-Drug Resistant Tuberculosis - came to the fore. Multi-Drug Resistant TB (MDR-TB) had been increasing and in 2003, Eli Lilly and Company globally

advocacy tools and technology to focus global resources on prevention, diagnosis and treatment.

Lilly Speke doubled its plant capacity with a £5 million investment to stem the tide until the benefits of the Lilly MDR-TB partnership would

**Top:** *Two old company delivery vans in Speke, 1966.* **Left:** *Opening of a new facililty in May, 2011.* **Above:** *An operator at work in today's Fermenter House.*

the site announced their change in product portfolio to take account of that capability as they moved to become an Elanco-focussed site. Elanco, established in 1954 is the animal healthcare division of Eli Lilly and Company and is a world leader in developing animal health products and services that enhance animal health, wellness and performance. As demand for one of the site's fermented products continues to grow, the site has called upon that significant expertise with scientific, engineering and manufacturing teams working hard to support increased output.

allow other countries to manufacture this life-saving medicine for themselves.

The initiatives of the Lilly MDR-TB Partnership all have one thing in common: improved care for some of the world's most vulnerable people, delivered in a sustainable manner that builds capacity within the communities where it is needed the most. As a result, Capreomycin production at Speke ceased in November, 2010.

The company's high reputation does not rest solely on its production strengths: it also aims to be a caring and responsible employer, and one which is part of the local community. The Company has a rich history of 'giving back' and each year runs a number of 'Day of Service' events supporting the community in which it operates. Recent activities have included providing the labour and funds for a garden makeover in Alder Hey hospital, renovating an external area at Marie Curie Hospice, work at the Dog's Trust and creating a community allotment. This is in addition to the financial support given to numerous charities and support for local schools.

Looking back at the site's history, they began their involvement in making animal healthcare products five decades ago and their knowledge in specialist active pharmaceutical manufacture as well as their biotechnology expertise coupled with scientific innovation is well recognised within the Corporation. In 2010,

Although an Elanco site the Lilly values of Respect for People, Integrity and Excellence hold as true for Elanco as for any division of Eli Lilly. Staff take pride in the brand, providing trusted solutions for their many customers.

Eli Lilly and Company's heritage is one that not only Eli Lilly himself would have been thrilled with, but also one which every person who has been involved with the Company can take equal pride and pleasure and that pride is sustained and continued as the site changes and thrives against a backdrop of innovation and experience.

*Above:* One of Lilly's Day of Service at the garden makeover in Alder Hey hospital. *Below:* Staff pictured for a Fun Run organised by the company in April, 2011, to raise funds for victims of the Japan earthquake.

# Bibby Line Group - Navigating the World

As an independent, family run business for over two hundred years the Liverpool-based Bibby Line Group has been consistently successful in the toughest world markets, navigating every kind of upheaval and challenge.

Historically, the company's main activities were founded in owning, operating and managing ships, but those activities have evolved down the years, turning the Bibby Line of today into a dynamic group of companies.

Throughout its history Bibby Line Group has maintained a reputation for high quality services conducted with integrity and safety and these values are as evident today as they were two centuries ago.

Today, Bibby Line Group is still based in Liverpool, UK, but it is also a truly global business - and every hour of every day, somewhere across the world Bibby Line Group will be at work.

The rise and decline of the British Empire, the Napoleonic and Boer Wars, the opening of the Suez Canal, the First and Second World Wars and the Falklands conflict have all affected the development of Bibby Line Group. Some events brought misfortune and loss; others brought opportunity and profit. Many shipping companies once based in Liverpool have either moved away from the city or have long since ceased to trade, but the Bibby Line has always been located in Liverpool. The first Bibby ships were wood and sail but the company moved quickly into iron and steam, pioneering such developments as the straight stem, steering from the bridge, and the tandem cabin.

**Top:** The *Mary Bibby* one of the Company's early wood and sail ships, pictured in Liverpool waters. **Left:** An egg and spoon race postcard from 1898. **Above:** A breakfast menu from the Yorkshire, one of Bibby Line's passenger liners

John Bibby of Liverpool first became involved in ship owning in 1801. The company he founded in 1807 has since then passed through dramatic changes of fortune, being inextricably linked with many of the major events and developments of the last two centuries.

During the middle of the 19th century the Bibby name became well established: Bibby Line steamers trading in the Mediterranean were so frequently met by other ships when traversing the sea that they were commonly known as Bibby's milestones.

Between 1859 and 1921 most of the Bibby Line ships were built by the Belfast shipyard Harland and Wolff.

In the late 19th century the tradition was established of naming Bibby Line vessels after English shire counties, a tradition which still persists to this day. It was these ships, built by Harland and Wolff, which began the liner service to Rangoon and Colombo for which the company became well known. Shortly afterwards began Bibby's long connection with carrying British troops overseas. Many servicemen recall with genuine affection the Bibby Line troop ships in which they sailed for India, Egypt, and the Far East. Most recently, servicemen were housed on Bibby accommodation barges in the Falklands.

By August 1914 on the outbreak of the Great War the Bibby Line fleet consisted of seven well-equipped steamers, five of which were less than ten years old, maintaining Bibby Line's reputation for a first class fleet. The war interrupted building work on the fleet's second *Lancashire* which was not delivered until 1917. The *Oxfordshire* was the first British merchant ship to be requisitioned, two days before war was declared. She was equipped as a hospital ship and served until March 1918, carrying over 53,000 wounded and traveling over 172,000 miles. The only loss suffered by the Bibby Line was the *Worcestershire* which sank in February 1916 with the loss of two lives after hitting a mine.

After the 1914-18 war business boomed. The Company was so confident of continued expansion in the Burma trade that it placed orders for two more cargo vessels. However, in 1921 the freight market suffered a collapse followed by a prolonged decline. Disputes in the coal industry raised the price of coal and restricted its supply. The Bibby Line adapted most of its existing vessels to oil, which proved to be both cheaper and

**Top:** Founder, John Bibby. **Below:** The *Shropshire* on Burma service in 1891.

more efficient, and ordered two new vessels with diesel motor engines. Another problem was competition from foreign fleets, especially those of the USA and Japan, which had been relatively unscathed by war.

Worst of all was the dire state of trade during most of the 1920s and 1930s. In 1929 over four and a quarter million tons of British shipping were laid up because of a lack of profitable work.

Even so the Bibby Line performed better than many other British shipping companies; new vessels were ordered as part of a plan to maintain a modern fleet. Eight new ships were ordered during the inter-war period, five of them at the most opportune time when building costs were low. The Bibby Line, during this period, had an outstanding service record with schedules rarely broken.

The Company moved to new offices on the seventh floor of the Martin's Bank Building, in Water Street, in 1932 and ceased its involvement in produce broking.

The Second World War began In 1939 with the immediate entry of Bibby Line's *Devonshire* into active service. Because she had been built for peacetime work she was too slow to keep up with North Atlantic and Mediterranean convoys and so she spent her time in less dangerous spheres of the war. Bibby Line suffered only two losses. The most serious was the *Yorkshire*, torpedoed while in convoy. She sank in nine minutes with the loss of 33 passengers and 25 crew. The other ship lost was the *Shropshire* and many others were victims of enemy action to some degree.

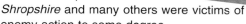

At the end of the war transportation and repatriation of troops kept several Bibby Line vessels occupied during most of 1945. Bibby Line's successful management of its trooping contracts gained them a contract in 1947 for the carriage of emigrants to Australia.

But, just as after the First World War, conditions were difficult. Labour was scarce and workers increasingly militant, with stoppages costing the company dear. There was a severe shortage of experienced officers, particularly engineers. Air travel would provide competition in years to come, but until the 1960s airliners could carry only small numbers of passengers. The advent of the jumbo jet, however, led to the demise of the ocean-going passenger trade. The work of

**Top:** The *Lancashire*, pictured off New Brighton in 1899. **Left:** Crew on Bibby's private yacht *Jason* during World War I. **Above:** Advertising for Bibby Line Sunshine Tours to the East.

carrying Imperial officers and staff declined as Britain withdrew from her Empire. Trade in Burma was slow to recover, and in 1965 Bibby Line had to withdraw its long-running passenger services from Rangoon and Colombo.

The introduction of National Service had meant that the Line's long association with trooping could continue. When it ended in 1962, however, the troops who were still required overseas were taken by air because this was so much quicker. Bibby Line did receive compensation, though, from the Government for the termination of trooping contracts before their due dates, which for a while provided a valuable annual source of revenue.

The disappearance of the Burma trade and the cessation of trooping work meant that Bibby Line had to find a new role in the shipping world. Derek Bibby began putting his own plans into action and taking advantage of a general upturn in the shipping world after the retirement of his father, Sir Harold Bibby. In partnership with the Bristol City Line the Company built two ships to trade between Britain and the Canadian Lakes. Trooping compensation was invested in new ships.

As a result Bibby Line was able to take part in the container revolution through the acquisition of Bristol City Line. It also now entered the emerging gas-shipping business almost by

**Above:** The second *Lancashire*, built in 1917. **Below left:** Sir Derek Bibby 1922- 2002 (5th Generation). **Below:** The *Yorkshire* in 1975 was the first purely oil tanker in the Bibby Line fleet.

The Board had decided to diversify to reduce reliance on the highly cyclical shipping markets and entered the offshore business. It invested a 20% stake in a semi-submersible accommodation platform, the *Safe Holmia*, in the North Sea.

Involvement with floating accommodation was a good investment over the next few years. Another bright spot was the Company's first outside management contract obtained in 1984 from the Shipping Corporation of Trinidad and Tobago for two methanol ships.

Bibby Line had gained its third Queen's Award for Exports in 1982. However, ships continued to be sold and the market remained depressed. There were many redundancies both at sea and on shore.

accident. Derek Bibby was invited to buy an LPG (Liquefied Petroleum Gas) carrier originally built for a charter which had fallen through. The LPG trade performed well, and Bibby Line ordered a second vessel.

It had been company policy never to borrow money but Derek Bibby changed all that. In the 1960s shipping companies were offered cheap credit and long term loans. Using these facilities Bibby Line developed a fleet of more than twenty ships. Charter work dominated the Bibby Line's activities and the Company had a spread of vessels operating in general cargo and gas carrying.

The Company received the Queen's Award for Export Achievement in 1972 yet soon Derek Bibby's twenty ships were in commission with nothing much to do. The depression of the Seventies was prolonged and painful and a total of seven Bibby Line ships were laid up, but because of the growth in its fleet the Bibby Line had received its second Queen's Award for Export Achievement in the previous year.

Following the launch of the *Staffordshire* in 1977 Bibby Line did not take delivery of another new ship for twelve years. 1978 was a crippling year with Bibby Line struggling to repay massive loans, in particular to the French.

The freight market was dreadful, with third party bankruptcies and bad debts galore. Changes made by the 1984 Finance Act found ship-owners paying tax despite making trading losses.

Bibby Line bought the *Safe Dominia* from the liquidators of Consafe with whom they had invested in the *Safe Holmia*, renaming it the *Bibby Venture* which, like the *Bibby Resolution*, was on contract to the Ministry of Defence in

**Top left:** Inspection by Bibby Ship Management. **Left:** A Costcutter store, part of Bibby Retail Services. **Above:** At work in Bibby Financial Services.

the Falklands, the first coastel the company owned.

Sir Derek Bibby was now succeeded as Managing Director by Simon Sherrard. Within its Marine Division Bibby also now established an important position in the worldwide transportation of chemicals through a part ownership of an Australian operator, Botany Bay, and direct ownership of a fleet of parcel tankers. In addition, it expanded its activities in the offshore oil and gas industry, in particular through the ownership and operation of jack-up platforms for accommodation and production purposes.

Bibby Line has been in existence for over 200 years and would not have survived over such a long period without a continuing commitment to the service of its clients. In 1989 the name of the business was changed to Bibby Line Group Limited, reflecting the broader range of activities the company was involved in.

Today, the business is managed by Sir Michael Bibby who, under the chairmanship of Simon Sherrard, has grown the business into a £1b turnover company, operating in over 20 countries, in a number of diverse sectors including financial services, logistics, shipping and ship management, offshore project management, retail, health and safety advisory services, woodland burials and construction equipment hire.

Bibby Line Group celebrated its bicentenary in 2007 and is proud to be a business built on lasting values. It is a company truly 'powered by its people'. Without the commitment to nurture long term relationships with its stakeholders it would not be the successful business one sees today. Bibby Line Group will continue to grow by making good investments in businesses and ensuring that there are high calibre management teams in place to develop them. In 1899 Arthur Bibby said "Our duty is.....to conduct business with every care and energy of which we are capable". And whilst the Bibby Line Group of today may look very different than it did over a century ago, the values held by the company then still remain true to this day.

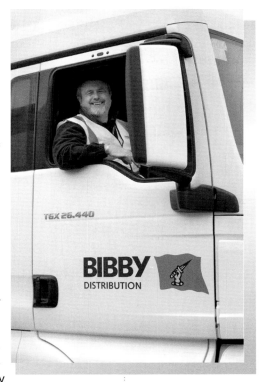

**Above:** Bibby Distribution. **Below:** The *Bibby Sapphire*.

# Jaguar Land Rover - A Green Future

Car manufacturing at the award-winning Halewood plant is once again experiencing the green shoots of growth, as the site prepares itself for an exciting new chapter in its recent history as a producer of premium British cars. Established as a key manufacturing location for the Jaguar Land Rover luxury car group, Halewood is gearing up to begin production of the latest addition to the Land Rover fold, the stunning new Range Rover Evoque.

The fruit of a £400 million development project, the exciting new Range Rover Evoque is being produced at Halewood alongside the highly popular award-winning Land Rover Freelander 2. To support the launch of the new model in 2011, Jaguar Land Rover set about recruiting more than 1,000 engineers, supervisors and production operators the previous year, so that the plant was totally ready to deliver the first vehicles to the market with its customary exceptional levels of quality and attention to detail.

Based on the iconic LRX concept car which caused such a stir on the motor show circuit when it was first presented in 2008, the Range Rover Evoque is the smallest, lightest and most fuel-efficient Range Rover ever produced. This green new vehicle is destined to expand and revitalise the global appeal of the Range Rover marque, and will be shipped from Halewood to more than 160 countries worldwide, with around 85 percent of production being exported.

Customers will have the choice of two distinctive versions: the stunning coupé model, which precisely mirrors the concept car design, and the stylish 5-Door, which adopts a slightly higher rear roofline for extra practicality and greater family appeal. This may be a smaller, greener Range Rover, but it stays true to the core values which customers have come to expect from the brand. The Evoque provides premium levels of craftsmanship, luxury, performance and renowned Land Rover all-terrain capability, but in a more compact package.

The Halewood site is no stranger to being a trailblazer for leaner, greener luxury vehicles. A couple of years earlier in 2008, the plant began production of the Freelander 2 TD4_e, the world's first SUV to feature an intelligent stop/start system which reduced both fuel consumption and CO2 emissions.

The innovative stop/start system only served to enhance the popularity of the Freelander 2, which was firmly established as Land Rover's top selling vehicle after its introduction in late 2006. Just 17 months after production started, Halewood shipped the 100,000th Freelander 2

**Top:** *The Range Rover Evoque Coupe. This stunning vehicle was built using advanced technology to deliver sporty performance together with the lowest fuel consumption of any Range Rover to date.* **Left:** *Employees pictured with the 250,000th Land Rover Freelander 2 produced at Halewood.* **Above:** *The Freelander 2 TD4_e.*

For Jaguar, this meant establishing a new manufacturing plant in addition to their facilities at Coventry, which had been home to Jaguar since before the war. The company injected £300 million into an imaginative refurbishment programme designed to completely revitalise and reshape the old plant. The refurbishment was essential for future success, as for 30 years Halewood had been producing Ford Escorts and it was critical that quality levels were raised to produce a premium sports saloon like the Jaguar. The refurbishment included replacing most of the former production facilities with the latest state-of-the-art equipment.

to a customer in the city of Surgut, located on Russia's Central Siberian Plateau. The destination of the vehicle reflected that while demand remained strong in traditional markets like the UK, there was booming interest across the world, and particularly in key emerging markets such as Russia, China and the Middle East.

Even as Halewood employees were involved in building the first Freelander 2 prototypes back in 2004, the plant was enhancing its environmental credentials by winning a series of awards – including Waste Minimiser Award, Environmental Business of the Year, and Environmental Best Practice Award – in recognition of considerable reductions in the consumption of energy, raw materials and water, and for waste minimisation.

Halewood provided all the major production facilities on one site: the main elements of press shop, body construction, paint shop and the trim and final assembly lines were laid out in an organised, linked manner next to one another to guarantee a smoothly flowing production line.

To further enhance efficiency, a new supplier park was created alongside the plant in co-operation with the Speke Garston Development Company and English Partnerships. The Boulevard Industry Park created about 500 jobs and enabled important suppliers such as Conix, Lear, Infast, Stadco and Visteon to manufacture components on Jaguar's doorstep. This seamless supplier network feeds components and sub-assemblies into the production line in an efficient and 'just in time' process.

### Halewood transformation

Halewood's role as a key source for premium Jaguar Land Rover vehicles dates back to its first associations with Jaguar at the end of the 20th century. The Jaguar connection sparked a complete transformation within Halewood, and the site would never be the same again.

While Halewood was operating as a Ford plant, there had been some production of Jaguar body panels at the site during the 1990s. However, approaching the new millennium, Jaguar revealed plans which would cement a major change for the plant. The company announced that it was introducing a new compact sports saloon known as the X-Type – the smallest car that Jaguar had produced in 30 years – and in 1998 it was confirmed that Halewood had won the manufacturing contract.

*Top left:* The refurbished administration building after completion in 2001. *Above:* Welding on the X-Type production line *Below:* The Jaguar X-Type nearing the end of the production line.

Word soon spread that there was something fresh and approachable about this company's style, without losing its sense of purpose and resolve. Even to a casual visitor the difference was immediately visible in the working environment. Halewood became a cleaner and more pleasant place to be, helping raise morale and improve quality, self-esteem and safety. When the last Ford left Halewood in 2000 it had become the 'Escort with Jag quality'.

Training played a critical role in the transformation. The technical training centre had the responsibility for educating apprentices, but the company's training of the workforce went much further. The close working relationship with Liverpool John Moores University was an important factor, providing appropriate courses for shop floor workers, engineers and managerial staff, some of them to degree level. As the plant moved into Jaguar production all employees underwent extensive retraining to equip them with the up to date knowledge that enabled them to adapt to the demands of building a top notch quality car.

The working culture at Halewood was dramatically changed in line with the transformation of the production processes. A programme designated as 'The Halewood Difference' was instituted, under the guidance of Senn Delaney Leadership, a top consultancy firm. Within 18 months of its launch in December 1998 there was a 20 per cent rise in productivity under the new management team that had David Hudson as Plant Operations Director.

Hudson had a reputation for making things happen and he refused to allow problems to fester. People were encouraged to bring those problems to him rather than let them remain unspoken or be part of a whispering campaign. Employees were encouraged to be part of the change and to play a role within the reshaping needed at Halewood so that they were contributing to what was happening and did not feel that they were having something foisted upon them. Issues were dealt with head on.

In total during the launch period, over one million hours of training, most of it on site, was given to the workforce, averaging some 350 hours for each and every employee. This had the effect of recharging the workers' batteries as well as those under the bonnets of the X-Types that began to roll off the assembly lines in February 2001.

### Jaguar returns to the North West

For Jaguar, the decision to establish a production base at Halewood marked a return to its historical roots in the North West of England. The company's founder William Lyons was born in Blackpool in 1901, and his early ventures in the automotive industry were based in that area.

Lyons had originally worked as a car salesman in the pioneering days of motoring, and satisfied his love of speed with a variety of nippy motorbikes. One of his neighbours,

**Top left and inset:** *Staff training at the the technical training Academy.* **Above:** *Jaguar's founder, Sir William Lyons.* **Left:** *A Lyons Swallow Sidecar.*

Coventry, the very heartland of the motor industry in this country. An alliance was forged with the Standard Motor Company that saw Lyons manufacturing and marketing his own cars, fitted with Standard engines and other components.

By now his ambitious and revolutionary ideas were about to send him along a path that would put his cars at the top of every person's ideal shopping list. Lyons had a new chassis ready and a magnificently powerful six cylinder overhead valve engine, capable of delivering 2.5 litres of

William Walmsley, had a similar passion for whizzing along the roads leading into the coastal resort. In a modest venture Walmsley had begun to produce sidecars. After purchasing one of these Lyons persuaded his neighbour to join forces with him in a business partnership. In 1922 their Swallow sidecar was an immediate hit.

Despite his personal preference for motorbikes Lyons was a shrewd enough businessman to realise that four-wheeled transport was where the major profits lay. He decided to move into car manufacture and used an Austin Seven chassis as the base for the first stylish body that he produced. The Austin Seven Swallow was introduced to the nation in 1927, generating one order of 500 models from a London distributor.

Lyons' little Blackpool factory was a victim of its own success, being too small to be able to cope with demand. Within a year the Swallow company had relocated to

*Top left:* The launch of the SS Jaguar in 1935. **Above:** Whitley bombers, essential wartime production at Jaguar's Coventry site. **Below:** The C-Type at Le Mans in 1953.

earth were shifted, but not without controversy as two ancient moated sites, the Old Hutt and Wright's Moat, were destroyed in the process. The gigantic nature of the work can be gauged from considering some of the figures involved. Structural steel weighed 40,000 tons, 300,000 tons of concrete was needed, 4 million bricks used, 2 million square feet of roofing erected and 50,000 gallons of paint applied. Little wonder that the cost of the initial operation came to £38 million.

By 1962, the training of the first recruits to the new workforce had commenced using a hangar at the airport as a training centre. The official opening took place a year later on 8 March, 1963, and the honour of being the first car to see the light of day at Halewood fell to a lime green Ford Anglia 105E De Luxe. When Ford production finished 37 years later in July 2000, well over 6

unbridled power. An elegantly striking saloon body topped off the new concept in luxury and performance. Lyons called the new car the SS Jaguar.

By the start of the war production of the new range of Jaguar cars had reached 5,000, and in the post-war period the company went from strength to strength. Lyons introduced a string of iconic Jaguar products, many of which gained countless successes in motorsport, including spectacular victories in the 24 Hours Le Mans race.

### Production starts at Halewood

In the same decade that William Lyons was introducing the legendary E-Type, the Halewood plant began production, as the Ford Motor Company decided to locate its new manufacturing site on Merseyside. The creation of the plant brought new hope to an area which was suffering from high levels of unemployment.

The Halewood site was purchased from Liverpool Corporation and the British Transport Commission, and construction began in 1960. More than 2 million tons of

million vehicles had been manufactured in Halewood, including multiple generations of the top-selling Ford Escort.

*Top left: The 1962 SI 3.8 E-Type. **Above:** One of the first Ford Anglia's to leave the production line at Ford Halewood. **Bottom left:** The one millionth Ford Escort produced at the plant. **Below:** Celebrating the production of four million cars at Halewood.*

and care for the environment has remained at the highest level. At Halewood state-of-the-art spray booths use water based colours, reducing solvent emissions. New heater and incineration systems have yielded major reductions in carbon monoxide and similar noxious gases.

Although the finish of X-Type production at the end of the 2009 – with a total of over 350,000 examples built – marked the end of Jaguar manufacturing for the time being, the Halewood team can look forward to an exciting future as the

**Leader in lean, green manufacturing**

The start of Jaguar production at Halewood in 2001 marked the beginning of a new era at the plant, as it set about creating a new reputation as a centre of excellence for top quality, lean and green car manufacturing. The efforts of the Halewood team were recognised by Ford's internal auditors, who rated the plant as the leading operation worldwide for lean manufacturing in 2002, 2003 and 2004. External judges were also impressed, with the influential JD Power group rating the X-Type as having best-in-class paint appearance between 2003 and 2006, and awarding the plant the prestigious European Gold Plant Award in 2005 in recognition of the X-Type's excellent quality.

On-going investment in the site, including a significant development to prepare the plant for the Land Rover Freelander 2 in 2006, has ensured that production quality

global source for the stunning new Range Rover Evoque. With the new owners of Jaguar Land Rover, Tata Motors, setting an ambitious growth strategy for the company, Halewood is ready to play a central role in a green and successful future.

*Top left and above:* At work on Halewoods Freelander production line. *Below:* The Range Rover 5 Door Evoque's global reveal at the LA Auto Show.

# Merchant Taylors' Schools
## The Best Education for Life

**MERCHANT TAYLORS' SCHOOLS**

The desire to get a good education is an ancient and honourable one. Education has always been the key to a successful life. Because of that fact those who have found success in life almost invariably look back to 'the happiest days of their lives' and give due credit to the academic institutions which helped forge their characters.

For four centuries Merseyside folk have been fortunate in being able to obtain an excellent education locally, ever since the reign of James I.

Merchant Taylors' Schools (MTS) are a family of independent schools, each with an enviable reputation throughout Merseyside, the North West of England and the UK.

The famous schools in Crosby were founded as a grammar school for boys by John Harrison in 1620, the year in which the Pilgrim Fathers first settled in New England. Well known former pupils include Robert Runcie, Archbishop of Canterbury from 1980 to 1991, and the novelist Dame Beryl Bainbridge. Amongst the staff, playwright Terence Rattigan taught Classics at the Boys' school before writing the famous work 'The Winslow Boy'.

Between its founding and today the original school has become four schools: a combined co-educational prep and junior girls' school known as Stanfield, a boys' junior school, and two senior schools situated on separate sites - one each for boys and girls.

The schools today are led by a new Chair of Governors, Professor Peter Batey, appointed in 2011. Headmaster, David Cook, of the Boys' School joined in September 2005 and Louise Robinson, Headmistress of the Girls' School was appointed in 2006. Over the last four years the Junior Schools have seen two new Head of Schools with Mrs Janet Thomas looking after the Junior Boys' School and Miss Julie Yardley in charge of the Junior Girls and Mixed Infants section.

Single sex education is at the core of the schools, although boys and girls are taught in mixed classes up to Year 3.

The schools' founder, John Harrison, was a member of the Merchant Taylors' Company in London where he owned considerable amounts of land, as well as in Yorkshire, Berkshire and Essex.

*Top left:* The school crest. *Above left:* The old school, which was built in 1620 to house 60 boys, is still in use today as part of the girls' school library and six form study area. *Left:* The whole school pictured in 1871 outside the old school house. *Above:* Heads of Merchant Taylors' Schools, L-R: David Cook, Louise Robinson, Julie Yardley and Janet Thomas.

build and endow a free grammar school in his father's home village - for teaching, educating and instructing children and youth in the grammar and rules of learning forever.

On his death John Harrison left enormous assets, part of which was bequeathed to the Merchant Taylors' Company to act as Trustees for his school in Crosby, a role they would retain until 1910.

The 'Guild and Fraternity of St. John the Baptist, time out of mind called tailors and linen armourers of London' had been in existence since at least in 1300 when it was recorded that 'they chose Henry de Ryall to be their pilgrim'. Letters Patent of Edward III issued in 1327 record Royal acceptance of the Guild in its first Charter.

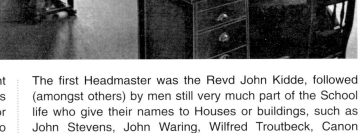

One legacy of those far-off days is the commonly used phrase 'all at sixes and sevens' meaning, 'all confused', or 'in disagreement'. The expression stems from the days when the Merchant Taylors' Company and the Merchant Skinners' Company were unable to agree amongst themselves as to which of the two ancient companies was the more senior – in 1484 Richard III was seeking to put his Guilds into ranking order; the Lord Mayor of London, one Billesden's, wise Solomon-like solution to the disagreement was that one year the Taylors' were ranked sixth, with the Skinners seventh, and vice versa the following year. This became known as the principle of 'sixes and sevens'. Of course this hardly resolved the question, but it provided a fitting solution to the disagreement!

The first Headmaster was the Revd John Kidde, followed (amongst others) by men still very much part of the School life who give their names to Houses or buildings, such as John Stevens, John Waring, Wilfred Troutbeck, Canon Samuel Armour, Thomas York, and Mark Luft.

The original building still stands in Crosby, as part of Merchant Taylors' Girls' School (MTGS) but is hidden from view by the newer buildings on Liverpool Road. Recently refurbished, the 1620s building is one of the oldest

Between 1512 and 1620 there had already been five schools and colleges established by Merchant Taylors' Company in England and Ireland – and now there was about to be a sixth.

John Harrison's father came from Great Crosby, and for several years before his death, John had it in mind to

*Top left and above:* Early 20th century classrooms. **Left:** An informal staff photograph of some members taken between 1904 and 1910. From bottom left, clockwise: Miss Mackenzie, Miss Mason, Miss Malpas, Miss Birchall, Mrs Burrows and Miss Mallaker.

buildings still in use in Sefton. In 2009 a new front entrance to the Girls' School was built. It provides a modern open frontage to the School. The Vitreum, as it is known, also contains an art gallery in the upper level which has seen many well known local artists present their exhibitions. The Patron of the Vitreum is Ben Johnson.

Meanwhile, during Canon Armour's headship (1863-1903), the School had the chance to expand and develop. It grew into an important day school, with the benefit of its ancient foundation, standing on an equal footing with the best ancient public schools in the country.

The Boys' School moved to an imposing new building in 1878. Since then this has been a famous landmark in Crosby, on the Liverpool to Southport A565 road. It is a fine example of Victorian architecture, with its imposing clock tower, which dominates the surrounding landscape.

Merchant Taylors' Girls' School was founded in 1888, having inherited the buildings from the boys' school that had moved 'up the road' in 1878. The then governing body was dilatory in providing for the 'new' school and it was only due to the insistence of James Fenning, the Master of the Worshipful Company of Merchant Taylors, that the girls' school was started. At the School's opening the female staff were all graduates, a fact that is very impressive considering that at the time only four universities were granting degrees to women! In June 1888 twelve pupils attended the school, by the 1920s this figure had grown to 300 and now has more than doubled to around 600. The continuing increase in pupil numbers enabled the purchase in 1911 of the adjoining house, 'The Mulberries', which doubled the existing space and still adds to the charm of the school. The jewel of the buildings, the now Grade II listed 1620s building (currently housing the library), has always dominated the surrounding area and new buildings. Two generous donations from a former headmistress ensured further development of facilities forming the basis of the current network of buildings.

The early girls' curriculum was based on a limited version of the boys', with little Mathematics or Latin - in case it taxed the female brain - and plenty of 'feminine' subjects such as singing and needlework to placate worries of producing only

*Top:* Merchant Taylors' Girls' School, Crosby, featuring a new front entrance. ***Above left:*** 6th Form boys in front of the famous clock tower. ***Below:*** A famous landmark in Crosby, the Victorian School was opened in 1878 by the Countess of Derby.

Academically Merchant Taylors' Schools have been consistently placed amongst the top schools in the North-West – they have also achieved outstanding sporting success in all disciplines. Though MTS has always had an excellent academic tradition, its pupils are now able to sample numerous extra-curricular activities.

As for younger students, Stanfield is the Merchant Taylors' mixed prep school and also the junior school for girls. It is located on its own site between the Boys' and Girls' Senior schools sites. It has been in this current position since 1946, and has during recent years seen major redevelopment with a new building. Pupils are able to use the senior schools' facilities such as the sports centre and swimming pool situated at the Boys' school.

'blue stocking' and thus almost guaranteed spinsterhood. The curriculum today, offering so much opportunity and variety, would have been hugely envied by the early girls.

Celebrating the centenary for the girls' in 1988 the school played host to Prince Andrew and Sarah Duchess of York. At this time the Centenary Hall was built and new facilities developed for science, modern languages and home economics.

Both Schools were inspected during 2010-11 receiving 'excellent' accreditations in the overall achievements of the pupils, their quality of personal development and the effectiveness of governance, leadership and management. The Schools' Early Years Foundation Stage (EYFS) provision was described as 'outstanding'.

Following the expansion of the Prep to two-form entry, in early 1998 Alan Hansen, former Liverpool football star (whose son started in the Preparatory department at MTS in 1988), opened the new classroom block and enlarged hall for the Prep - which was at the same time re-named as the Merchant Taylors' Junior Boys' School.

Throughout the twentieth century, the School has moved with the times - making the successful transition from Public School to Direct Grant, and in due course, to Independent status.

*Top left:* The Tennis Team, 1926. *Pictured from left to right, back row: Peggy Grant, Ethel Hiller-Hughes, Doris Gerrard, front row: Joan Williams (Vice Captain) Hazel Thornton (Captain) and Lillian Kenworthy.* **Left:** *Prince Andrew and Sarah Duchess of York's celebratory visit to the school in 1988.* **Above:** *Reception pupils from Stanfield.*

The abolition of the Government Assisted Places Scheme in 2002, which supported over 30% of the Schools' intake, was replaced by the introduction of an Assisted Places Scheme fully funded by the Schools, mainly through generous donations from alumni into the Schools' Bursary Fund.

The Girls' and Boys' Schools' have faced up to the future of competitive education, and succeeded in consistently maintaining some of the best academic results in the North West. During previous inspections the Schools have been commended with a glowing report as being outstanding in its many achievements, not just academically, but also in their many extra-curricular activities: music, drama, sport, Combined Cadet Force, and through the many societies which give pupils a chance to experience far more of life than just that inside the classroom.

As the Merchant Taylors' company's ancient Latin motto in the school crest says 'Concordia parvae res crescunt' - 'small things grow in harmony' - so the Schools' whole ethos is one in which a warm, and friendly atmosphere fosters the best which pupils have to offer, developing them to their full potential, and preparing them for the challenges of the modern world beyond. Today the modern schools' motto

however is in English - 'The Best Education for Life' - for most that personal preparation includes participation in such challenging sports and other extra-curricular activities as drama, music, rowing, sailing and the Combined Cadet Force where they have the opportunity of attending a variety of camps and courses, both in Great Britain and overseas. Both boys and girls are encouraged to take part in the Duke of Edinburgh Award Scheme, and many achieve success in Bronze, Silver and Gold awards.

The schools also play an active role in the local community; they carry out many fundraising activities for local charities such as Alder Hey and the NSPCC. During 2010 the Schools raised over £18,000 for local and national charities.

In September 2011 Merchant Taylors' Schools saw the opening of a new £5.5 million facility called the Ian Robinson Sports Centre. Located at the Boys' School site on Liverpool Road, this ambitious development designed by Buttress Fuller Alsop Williams Architects, will benefit all pupils from the family of

*Top left:* Pupils from the Junior Boys' School. *Left:* Sport is a big part of life at Merchant Taylors' - pictured are the under 13s netball champions. *Above:* Year 1 girls from Merchant Taylors' Girls Junior School - Stanfield pose for a photograph for the 1953 prospectus brochure.

Merchant Taylors' Schools, and will include a dance studio, fitness suite and a large indoor facility equipped to provide state-of-the-art facilities for rugby training, football, hockey, tennis, badminton and many other sports.

Leo Coligan, former Chairman of Governors, said at the time: "This exciting build underlines our confidence in the future of Merchant Taylors' Schools and their pursuit of excellence in all areas, academic and sporting, and our determination to provide the very best facilities for our boys and girls."

Alongside this new period of development for the Schools a new two-year campaign called Sporting Start was launched in 2010, marking the first milestone in a new ongoing period of fundraising. Between 2002 and 2008 the Schools successfully raised over £1 million to support the ongoing Bursary Fund. Following on from this the Governors set the objective of raising a further £1 million to secure that fund, as well as £1 million to invest in a number of capital build developments being made at the Schools over the current decade when the Schools celebrate their 400th Anniversary in 2020.

The title 'Sporting Start' refers to the opportunities the Bursary Fund provides, by giving a child a sporting start in life. As well as this it provides the theme for a celebration of the strong sporting tradition at the Schools that continues to this day with creation of the new Sports Centre.

For nearly 400 years MTS has been the best academic and all round independent school in the North West and the hope is it will continue for the next 400 years.

**Top left:** The under 15s rugby squad - winners of the Lancashire Cup. **Above left:** Young biathletes from the Junior Girls' School. **Below:** An artist impression of Merchant Taylors' new sports centre.

# Henry Bath & Son
## Conquering Commerce, with an Enduring Business

The Bath family motto is 'He Conquers Who Endures'. Today, Henry Bath & Son Ltd, based in Princes Parade, off St Nicholas Place, in Liverpool, has more than lived up to that motto. The firm first opened an office in Liverpool in Bentinck Street, along with associated metal warehouses, in 1875.

The Henry Bath Group is today a world-leading logistics provider, specialising in the storage and shipping of Exchange-traded metals and agricultural commodities around the world.

The Group operates in key port locations across the USA, Europe, Asia and the Middle East, providing its clients with a global platform of Exchange-approved storage depositories for holding, making and taking delivery of physical commodity products.

Henry Bath is licensed by the London Metal Exchange ('LME'), the London International Financial Futures and Options Exchange ('NYSE Euronext.Liffe') and the Intercontinental Exchange ('ICE') in New York to store and issue Exchange-traded Warrants (bearer documents of title) for commodities including aluminium, copper, zinc, lead, nickel, tin, aluminium alloy, steel billets, cocoa and coffee.

In recent years the Group has continued to develop its warehousing operations, particularly across Asia, as the trade flow of commodities that the business handles continues to shift East to feed the global manufacturing base.

In 2003 the LME listed new Henry Bath warehouses in the ports of Busan and Gwangyang in South Korea and in Dubai. In 2004 the Group opened commodity warehousing operations in Shanghai, Johor, Chicago and Antwerp. Continuing the pioneering spirit of the Company heritage, in 2008 Henry Bath was the first warehouse company to establish LME-approved storage facilities in Istanbul, Dubai, Johor and Incheon for the new LME steel contract, once again re-uniting Henry Bath with ferrous metals.

But who was Henry Bath? Who were his sons? And how did this Liverpool firm come to occupy its present globe-girdling position?

The Bath family history reaches back to 1216 when Sir Walter de Bath, Knight, became Sheriff of Devon during the reign of

*Top: Cutting ingots of tin at the turn of the Century. **Above:** Founder Henry Bath.*

Henry III. Henry Bath, a descendant of Sir Henry Bath, was a Cornishman born in Falmouth in 1776; he eventually founded a copper trading business after first training as a carpenter, working as a property developer, and later as an accountant for a business specialising in the Cornish copper trade.

Henry and his family were Quakers. He, like his father before him, became a member of the Society of Friends as the Quakers are officially known. The Friends or Quakers were a well respected non-conformist movement who at that time enjoyed considerable influence, not least in their opposition to slavery.

Quakers were famously hardworking and trustworthy. Armed with a good reputation, and a knowledge of metal trading between Cornwall and Wales, Henry now set up a business on his own account.

In 1820, four years after he relocated to Swansea, Henry Bath is recorded as 'preparing a yard... with many conveniences attending it', this most likely also included the wharf he had built. By 1822 he had become the agent for the Berehaven copper mines in Ireland, founded in 1812 by 'Copper' John Puxley and had established himself with some of the leading Swansea industrialists of the time. In Pigot's Directory of 1823 Henry is listed as an agent to Sir John Morris, who was most

notable as a coal magnate, but was also instrumental in the industrial development of Swansea through his participation in the building of canals and tramways.

In 1825 or 1826 Henry acquired the Landore Copper Works in partnership with R. J. Nevill, who was both a copper and coal baron and would later open the important London residential market to Welsh coal. The Landore smelting operation remained in their hands until 1837, when it was sold to Williams Foster & Co. At an unknown date Henry wrote to Lord Audley's agents, 'all the ores from England, Ireland, Scotland and Wales which are brought to Swansea for sale are under my care ... I have about 800 tons now on my wharf for sale ... My friend Mr. Puxley, for whom I am Agent, has been here lately, also my friend John Taylor has very lately spent a few days at my home.'

By 1822 Henry had already moved his headquarters to his wharf in Swansea (Bath's Copper Ore Yard in Bath Lane) and taken his son, Henry Bath II into partnership. Bath & Son would come to own and operate a fleet of vessels, and develop trade with Chile, exporting coal and returning with copper ore and sodium nitrates.

The Bath's business operation covered all aspects of the copper trade, including sampling the ore on arrival, weighing it, setting freights and landing charges, and finally arranging for its sale by the 'ticketing' process.

In 1846 Henry Bath II established the Swansea Iron Shipbuilding Company. Three years later, in 1849, he launched the steam yacht 'Firefly' intended for use on the coast of Chile. Many of their ships were built at Bideford in North Devon and were named after the letters of the Greek alphabet such as Alpha, Beta, Gamma Delta, Iota, Kappa, Epsilon, Theta and Zeta (built at Glasgow). The Hollywood actress, Catherine "Zeta" Jones, is named after the Henry Bath "Zeta" ship that was captained by her great grandfather. Other vessels' names were inspired by the novels of James Fennimore Cooper, author of 'Last of the Mohicans', including Scout, Hawkeye, Uncas,

*Top left:* Rose Hill, The Mumbles, Swansea, the home of Henry Bath. *Left:* The Alltyferin Estate, home to several generations of the Bath family. *Above:* Henry Bath II.

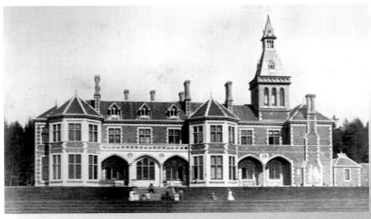

The Industrial Revolution had by now turned Britain from an exporter of base metals into a voracious importer and that meant long delivery times. Whereas the coffee houses had traded physical contracts, the new LME allowed merchants to forward-sell to guarantee their prices. Communication was becoming easier too – both physically, with the opening of the Suez Canal and development of steam ships, and electronically with the telegraph and, subsequently, the telephone. Delivery could be accurately forecast, and the LME's

Delaware, Pathfinder, Mohican and Deerslayer. There were also vessels called Henry Bath and City of Valparaiso. Records exist of all these barques, often referred to as 'Cape Horners' and as many as 30 ships formed the Bath fleet.

On a visit to Chile, Henry Bath II and his brother Edward met and married the two daughters of Charles Lambert another prominent Swansea shipbuilder and copper merchant. This association brought into the company copper smelting operations in Chile, at Coquimbo and Port Tennant, Wales.

Henry Bath II and brother Charles, who managed the fleet and copper yards, opened an office in London during the 1850s. Transactions were initially carried out there rather informally in various trading offices, and frequently over coffee, which was then very fashionable, in the Jerusalem Coffee House, just off Cornhill.

In January 1877 the London Metal Exchange ("LME") Company was formed to provide a more regulated forum for their transactions: its first venue was in a room over Christie's, the hat makers, whose premises were situated at number 4, Lombard Lane, London.

standard three month contract reflected transport times for copper from Chile and tin from Malaya.

With the opening of the London Metal Exchange the firm of Henry Bath & Son, a founder member of the Exchange, began to take on business with an increasingly widening international aspect.

The very first London Metal Exchange warrant was issued for 352 copper bars imported from New York into Liverpool on the vessel "Adriatic", on 20 December, 1883, by Henry Bath and remains to this day, completed of course, in the Company archives.

The formalised market proved highly successful, not least in resisting French-led attempts to corner the copper market in 1889. As Britain's self-sufficiency in tin and copper ended, an increasing number of European traders started using London, not only for the main metals, but to deal in antimony and quicksilver too, though this was outside the LME's remit.

*Top, both pictures:* Two of the Henry Bath ships; The Delta (top left) and The Zeta (top right). *Left:* A view inside the London Metal Exchange in its early days. *Above:* The first LME warrant.

Soon the Exchange had more than 300 members, forcing a move to a purpose-built site in Whittington Avenue, Leadenhall Market. However, there were fears that such a large membership was disorderly, and at the start of the new century, the Exchange's ruling committee imposed tougher regulations to reduce the numbers. This move enhanced the market's reputation and that of its members.

In 1890 the Government had recognised Henry Bath & Son's prominent role as a leading and founding member of the London Metal Exchange. To facilitate the process of handling and storing metals the Government passed a Special Act of Parliament which empowered Henry Bath & Son to issue transferable Certificates and Delivery Warrants

Liverpool FC's Anfield football stadium as the club's flag pole. Ironically this landmark project was also the year that Charles Bath died, the last of the founder's sons.

The outbreak of the First World War in 1914 almost ruined the business, and destroyed the wealth built up by its owners. Much of the Bath family investments were in Germany and in trade with Germany's allies.

The last of the Bath's with a direct involvement in the business died in 1921 a year after the firm became a limited company. Ownership passed to the Morrice and Anthony families.

After the Second World War the company diversified into buying and selling steel. It continued as a privately owned family firm until the early 1970s, when it was bought out by the British Bank of Commerce in Glasgow. In 1975 the

*Above: The SS Great Eastern in its final days before dismantling. Below: Cocoa storage in the late 19th century. Left: Unloading goods with the help of horse and cart.*

from their own office. An amendment to this bill updating the process was made in 1920 and remains in force today (the original Government Bills are still held in the company archive).

Meanwhile, in 1888, the company had a ship breaking business and bought The SS Great Eastern for £16,000. This had been the largest ship in the world at the time it was constructed, designed and built by the renowned engineer Isambard Kingdom Brunel. It was broken up and sold for scrap at its final resting place, Tranmere at Birkenhead. One of the ship's masts now stands at

warehousing operation, later sold, to maintain its strategic focus on the core business of storing Exchange-traded metals and other commodities.

In June 2005, Henry Bath & Son Ltd issued the first LME Warrant for plastics and in 2008 it was among the first LME-approved warehouse companies to store and issue warrants for the LME's new steel contract.

Today, Henry Bath & Son is approved by the world's premier commodity Exchanges, including the London Metal Exchange (LME), to issue Exchange-traded bearer documents (Warrants) for metals stored at the Group's

company became an important member of a major Australian mining group, MIM Holdings. It was later taken over by Metallgesellschaft (MG), a major German corporation for the purpose of physically handling and storing non-ferrous metals around the globe.

During the period 1995 to 1999 Henry Bath expanded its operations by acquisitions in Singapore and the USA. Additionally, Henry Bath added Rotterdam to its list of European operations and moved into the handling and storage of cocoa beans. In Liverpool a major programme of property development was undertaken for a general goods

*Top:* Unloading sodium nitrates in Liverpool from Chile. ***Above left:*** Copper trading at the LME in the 1950s. ***Above:*** Storing copper wire bars (used to manufacture electrical cable) in the 1980s.

Henry Bath has over 200 years of experience in storing and handling metals traded on the London Metal Exchange. The Company issued the first ever LME Warrant in 1883 and is still issuing Warrants to this day. Warehouse managers and staff are highly trained to understand the Exchange's regulations for storing and caring for the valuable stocks in Henry Bath warehouses. Long-standing experience, together with strong financial backing and parentage, provides clients with all the assurances they have a right to expect from a global commodity warehousing partner.

Meanwhile, the Bath family had an even older family motto than 'He Conquers Who Endures' – that other motto is Habere et Dispertire, Latin for 'To hold and to distribute'. Surely no words could more aptly define the firm of Henry Bath and Son in the 21st century.

facilities worldwide. The Exchanges continually audit operations to ensure the Group is meeting their rigorous standards and delivering a high quality service to customers year after year.

Henry Bath now operates in 19 key locations across the USA, Europe, Asia and the Middle East, providing customers with a comprehensive range of commodity storage services. The Group's global network of Exchange approved storage facilities at premier port locations gives its customers the ability to hold and deliver stocks from key distribution points around the world. Whatever the task, clients are assured the same high quality standard of

*Top:* A bird's eye view of the company's dockside premises. *Left:* Aluminium ingots stored in Henry Bath's storage facilities. *Above:* 8 Princes Parade, home of Henry Bath's Liverpool offices today. *Below:* Discharging metal ingots from a breakbulk ship.

warehousing services at all Henry Bath facilities around the globe. The Henry Bath branded Warrants and Warehouse Receipts are recognised by the world's major international banks as financeable documents, allowing customers to readily finance their physical metal stocks. Sophisticated stock control systems are employed for accurate real-time reporting and comprehensive state-of-the-art security systems are installed in all of the Company's warehouses to protect clients' valuable stocks.

# Nutricia - Advanced Medical Nutrition

I n 2010 the international foods group Danone made a £20m investment in Liverpool to upgrade its hi-tech medical foods manufacturing facility in Wavertree Boulevard.

The three-year improvements programme was centred on Nutricia Liverpool, part of Nutricia Advanced Medical Nutrition, previously known as SHS International before its acquisition by the Netherlands-based Medical Division of Danone (France).

The Nutricia business can trace its history in Liverpool back more than 120 years.

It is now part of the specialised healthcare unit of Danone which develops and manufactures medical nutrition for many types of consumers and patients at all stages of life, but particularly young children, the ill and the elderly.

Founded in the Netherlands in the town of Zoetermeer, Nutricia was originally a specialist in infant formulas. Laboratory-synthesised baby milk was produced to match the nutritional needs of different babies. In 1905 Nutricia pioneered the concept of specialised medical nutrition, developing special diet products such as low-sugar milk for diabetic patients and iodine-rich milk for those suffering from goitre.

In the modern era, Nutricia focused more intensely on the development of research based nutritional products. In 1946, it opened its first proprietary research department within its laboratories. Dieticians were hired in 1950 to provide medical information to doctors, nurses and other healthcare professionals. Scientific advances of the 1960s led to development of specialised nutritional products for hospitals, and the introduction of Nutri 2000 - a complete nutrition solution for the chronically ill with serious feeding problems.

In the 1990s, Nutricia acquired the highly specialised firms of SHS International (UK) and Milupa (Germany), gaining new expertise in areas such as Inborn Metabolic Disorders and severe Cow's Milk Allergy. With the UK baby food brand Cow & Gate, these businesses were brought together under the umbrella of Numico.

The firm of SHS International (UK) traced its Liverpool roots back to 1879 and to the local firm of Powell & Scholefield Ltd from which SHS grew, and became a separate company in 1991.

Henry Ernest Scholefield and his father-in-law Richard Powell formed a partnership manufacturing chemicals in Manchester for the brewing industry. In 1889 the

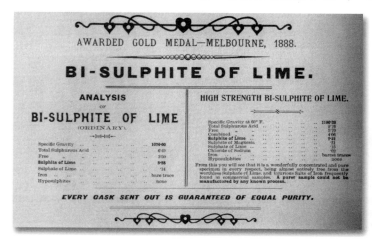

AWARDED GOLD MEDAL—MELBOURNE, 1888.

## BI-SULPHITE OF LIME.

ANALYSIS
OF
BI-SULPHITE OF LIME
(ORDINARY).

HIGH STRENGTH BI-SULPHITE OF LIME.

EVERY CASK SENT OUT IS GUARANTEED OF EQUAL PURITY.

**Top left:** *Henry Ernest Scholefield.* **Above:** *Richard Powell.* **Left:** *Analysis of Bi-sulphate of lime.*

partnership bought 38, Queensland Street, Liverpool, for £1,000, an address which included two houses and their orchards. By then Richard Powell had been ill for some years and took no further active part in the business.

Henry himself allegedly chopped down the trees to fire the 'pots' which were then, and even after the Second World War, used in the production of sulphurous acid and bisulphate of lime – although it is more than likely that the wood was turned into charcoal for use in the process.

If Summer Comes—-

**S**hould summer come at all this year
**U**nusual troubles may appear.
**L**et not worry cloud your mind
**P**erhaps if you would try to find
**H**ow others turn out brews O.K.
**O**n any hot and sultry day,
**S**o may you learn that yeast and beer
**I**s kept by them both pure and clear
**T**heir troubles nil, their outlook bright
**E**nsured by the use of "SULPHOSITE."

*Sole Makers:*

**POWELL & SCHOLEFIELD LTD.**
**LIVERPOOL, 7.**

Although a small business – the records suggest fewer than a dozen employees – the partnership was not content to depend solely on the home market. Special sales efforts were directed towards the colonies and good trading relationships were established with a number of overseas breweries. Hydro-sulphate of lime was exhibited with other products at the Great Melbourne Exhibition of 1889 and was awarded a Gold Medal. As 'Sulphosite' it was still being used by brewers almost a century later.

During the years around the turn of the century P&S made little further progress. No new products were developed and sales of existing lines declined. Victorian Britain had a striving, aggressively self-made quality but the Edwardian era which followed brought with it a desire for elegance and gracious living divorced from the harsh world of work. Henry Scholefield, following the fashion, moved from Edge Hill to Wavertree, and later out to the Wirral. Increasingly his life revolved around his home. Running the business was left to two professional managers Robert Allanson and Stanley Hacket Sears.

Both Robert Allanson and Stanley Sears had attended Dr Tate's College in Liverpool to learn chemistry. Sears would

take over the running of the factory and laboratory whilst Allanson would eventually concentrate on sales.

Arthur Scholefield, Henry's youngest son, joined the company in 1919 and soon a search for new products and opportunities was launched.

The partnership had become a limited company in 1910, prospering with the production of 'Hydrosalis' and 'Sulphosite'.

After recording record profits of £5,074 in 1920 Arthur Scholefield, Robert Allanson and Stanley Sears were all given shares in the company. In 1921 Robert Allanson became a Director. The following year both Arthur and his brother Stephen became Directors, with Arthur following his father as Chairman.

But despite the prosperity of the 1920s hard economic times lay ahead. The Government put a penny on the price of a pint of beer, whilst growing unemployment, short-time and cuts in wages forced working families to make economies; beer was a luxury many had to forego. Many small firms failed: P&S kept going, but no dividends were paid in 1931, 1932 and 1933.

Two things contributed to the firm's survival. One was the introduction by Arthur Scholefield of 'Moabrite' an industrial

*Above left: The gold medal awarded to Powell & Scholefield's Hydro-sulphate of lime at the Great Melbourne Exhibition of 1889. Left: Robert Allanson (far left) and Stanley Hackett Sears (left). Top right: An early Powell & Scholefield Sulphosite advert. Above: Arthur Scholefield.*

Meanwhile Mrs L W Scholefield, wife of Arthur Scholefield, had been made a Director in 1939. She worked in the laboratory where her particular job was mixing the 'Vitamin Yeast Food' – her enthusiasm for new ideas would have a significant impact on the firm's future.

Understanding the brewing process had been mastered in scientific terms and was now replacing the old rule of thumb. P&S hired its first graduate chemist and sent him to Birmingham University to study brewing science: Gordon Jones would eventually become the firm's Managing Director and see the company move into biochemicals.

Vitamin Yeast Food was a natural outgrowth of the brewing business, and of the company's increasingly able scientific staff. In the late 1950s the possibility of dietary treatment for some inherited medical conditions was being understood and the company was invited to manufacture a foodstuff free from the phenylalanine harmful to children suffering from Phenylketonuria (a rare condition in which a baby is born without the ability to properly break down the amino acid phenylalanine). The process developed in the Queensland Street laboratories would lead to the first of a long series of

cleaning product whose sales more than made up for the losses on Sulphosite. The cleaner came to the market just as the dairy industry was moving over to the large scale use of milk bottles, and many tons were sold both at home and abroad. The second thing was a complete reorganisation of the Board and an injection of capital from the younger members of the Scholefield family.

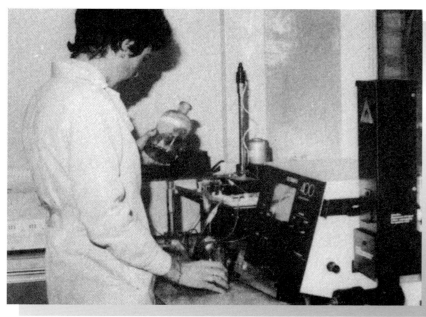

*Top left:* A 1930s laboratory. *Left:* Advertising for Moabrite. *Top right:* Mrs L W Scholefield. *Below:* Quality control laboratory instrumentation.

BRIGHTER BOTTLES
WITH
*Moabrite*
THE ALL EFFICIENT CLEANSER

Sole Makers
POWELL & SCHOLEFIELD. LTD
*Established 1879.*
EDGE HILL    -    LIVERPOOL

Moabite may have been good for the business. But it wasn't all good news. Men went home with their faces sore and bleeding after they had been working on a batch. Usually it was mixed in the yard, and the wind swirled the caustic particles about. 'Aye it kept you warm around the ears' was one worker's recollection.

In 1939 and 1940 premises at the corner of Cardwell Street and Sidney Place were acquired and added to the factory. One of the buildings was infested with fleas – so badly that men refused to work there until they were offered an extra five shillings a day to clear it out.

During the war years which followed Henry Ernest Scholefield died, soon to be followed by his wife and sister-in-law, bringing to an end the involvement of the first generation in the family firm.

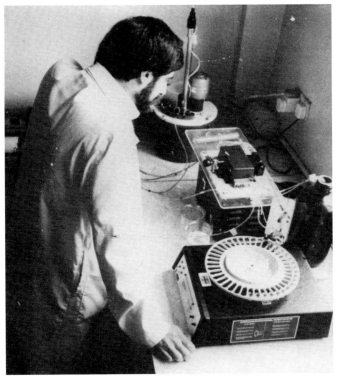

The company has a century of experience, producing a wide variety of products from niche, small volume products for individual cases through to bulk orders for patients across the world. Continual expansion and investment in new technology have ensured that Nutricia will continue to strive to provide the best possible service to its customers.

Research is at the heart of the company ethos; the long-term strategy is to translate concepts into new formulations that meet patients' needs. With its technical expertise and knowledge Nutricia is providing palatable and acceptable products to help improve patient compliance: its mission is to bring health through food to as many people as possible.

nutritional products with a medicinal use, and to the company's eventual incorporation within the Numico group.

Numico was in turn acquired in 2007 by Danone and renamed Nutricia Advanced Medical Nutrition. Nutricia's Human Nutrition Research team, now part of Danone Research, is one of the largest in the world, with over 200 nutritional scientists, molecular biologists and chemists, all working to create innovations at the forefront of medical nutrition.

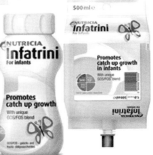

Nutrition is increasingly recognised as playing an important role in modern health care provision and advanced medical nutrition is key to effective disease management. Nutritional intervention can improve clinical outcomes and give patients a greater chance of recovery and independence, whilst relieving the clinical and financial burdens of health authorities.

*Top left: Papain Assay on an Auto-Analyser. Top right: Ameno-Acid Analyser, 1979. Centre: A selection of Nutricia products, Anamix: for a safe diet and a normal life for people with in born errors of metabolism, Infatrini: resolves allergy problems and promotes catch-up growth in infants and young children and Nutilis: targeted nutrition to support specific disease treatments. Below left and below: Nutricia's innovations rely on breakthrough research in nutrition with evidence-backed products delivering clear health benefits to patients.*

# MERSEYSIDE FIRE & RESCUE SERVICE
## Making Merseyside Safer

The Fire and Rescue Services in Merseyside have a long and honourable history. Fire became a big problem in the 19th century as buildings got ever larger. Following a particularly bad conflagration at Lancelot Hey in 1833, when many warehouses and homes were destroyed, a Liverpool city fire brigade was established the following year.

Other towns on Merseyside followed; Birkenhead formed its own police-fire brigade in 1837, but, as with Wallasey, Southport and St Helens, it relied upon co-operation with larger brigades if efficient fire fighting was to be carried out.

By the 1860s, horse-drawn steam-powered pumps were seen fighting fires in Liverpool's streets. After much experimentation, mechanically propelled fire engines were in regular use in Liverpool and indeed throughout Merseyside by 1910.

By the 1930s modern looking fire appliances were widely available to fight fires in Merseyside. It was just as well given the conflagration which lay just around the corner courtesy of Herr Hitler and the Luftwaffe.

Merseyside was a strategic target for the Luftwaffe as it contained Liverpool, Bootle, Wallasey and Birkenhead which comprised the most important port complex serving the vital sea routes to and from the USA and Canada. Severe bombing in late 1940 was followed by further raids in early 1941 culminating in the infamous May Blitz during the first week of May 1941 with over 1,250

civilians killed on one night alone. Bootle became the most bombed town in the UK and Merseyside as a whole was the most seriously bombed area outside London.

In August 1941 the Auxiliary Fire Service, which had been formed in 1938 and had grown to over 6,000 men and women on Merseyside alone, along with the professional brigades across the UK were nationalised. So for the next seven years the National Fire Service provided cover for the people of Merseyside. In 1948, control of the Service was returned to the local brigades but now there was strong central government control and regulation incorporating the hard lessons learned in 1940 and 1941.

Many more years would have to pass, however, before women would join as operational members of the Fire Service. It would take a social revolution before the name 'fireman' would be changed to 'fire officer'. Other changes would be less obvious. Many readers will recall 'fire engines' still mounting wooden ladders, firemen sporting fireman's axes on their belts, and the furious ringing of a fire engine bell, before bells were replaced by today's far more penetrating claxons.

Merseyside County Fire Brigade was formed on 1 April, 1974. It comprised 34 fire stations and incorporated the former City of Liverpool, County Boroughs of Bootle, Southport, Wallasey,

*Top left:* Mather Avenue fire station in the 1950s. **Below:** A Wallasey Dennis engine from the 1970s.

Birkenhead and St Helens fire brigades as well as three stations from Cheshire and seven from Lancashire County. Unusually for a local authority brigade, it provided cover for Liverpool's Speke Airport.

The long hot summer of 1976 saw a huge increase in the volume of calls, placing a great strain on the brigade's resources. The fleet of differing appliances inherited from the eight brigades was ageing, and many now became even more worn. Eventually 12 of the Bedford Emergency pumps known as 'Green Goddesses' were borrowed from the Home Office store at Blackpool; in addition a number of vans manned by staff officers were put to use.

In the aftermath, the Chief Officer, Sid Rankin, was faced with the need to replace virtually the entire front line fleet of pumps. Within a two year period no less than 30 Dennis R Series Water tender ladders (WrL) and the first ten of 27 RS Series WrLs were brought into service.

Two huge fires in the St John Precinct Shopping centre were dealt with in 1977 and 1979. Then the 1980s saw riots break out in Liverpool 8, and once again the Brigade was exposed to a period of frenetic activity.

Liverpool had for over a century been linked to the cotton trade and hence cotton fires whether on-board ships or in warehouses were frequent. This remained the case in the 1970s and into the 80s, but gradually this part of Merseyside's past became only a memory.

In 1982 responsibility for providing cover at the airport was handed over to the airport's own service. Meanwhile, since its creation, the Brigade had been organised on a Divisional basis, in five Divisions: North, South, East, West and Central responsible for providing Fire Cover and Fire Prevention services within their respective areas. In September 1992, after a major review a new structure was put in place, those hierarchical Divisions were abolished, and replaced by pan-Merseyside Commands the principal ones being Operations and Fire Safety.

The 1990s were turbulent times on Merseyside with much industrial unrest including a National Fire Strike. In 2002 Tony McGuirk, who had transferred into Merseyside from Essex Fire and Rescue Service six years earlier, was appointed CFO. Gradually significant changes were introduced that saw dramatic falls in the numbers of fire deaths and injuries, down from over 30 each year in the 1980s to between five and ten per year today.

At the same time visits to conduct Home Fire Safety Checks in people's homes were introduced, and now over 100,000 are regularly undertaken each year. Community Work has become core to the Service's day-to-day work.

*Top left:* A St Helens Leyland Water Tender, 1970s. *Above:* Dennis RS Water Tender Ladder *Below:* A 2010 Merseyside Fire and Rescue Service Scania Rescue Pump.

A change from Dennis fire appliances, which since its formation had been the core of the Brigade's fleet of front line pumps, began in 2000 with a gradual switch to Scania-chassied Rescue Pumps. These carried not only the equipment previously found on a WrL but also hydraulic cutting and spreading equipment for use at Road Traffic Collisions.

The Service was the pioneer in the introduction of fire-fighting motorbikes in the UK with two bikes introduced for trials in 2010. These followed on from the Small Fires Units brought in to deal with rubbish and abandoned vehicle fires.

The digital revolution has been embraced on Merseyside with mobile data terminals being fitted on all Rescue Pumps to provide site and risk information, and a new Incident Ground Management Unit with state-of-the-art secure wireless links to tough book-laptops for Sector Commanders replacing paper messages at incidents.

A MAN 4-wheel drive chassis has recently been purchased; this not only has an off-road capability but also incorporates a lifting rig which can be used to lift trapped animals.

The formation of a charity linked to community work and to efforts to reduce anti-social behaviour and deliberate fires has enabled significant outside funding to be attracted which would otherwise not be available to the Service. The involvement of local communities in projects is seen as imperative for their long term success.

With the Port of Liverpool at the heart of the city Merseyside Fire and Rescue maintains significant marine capabilities. Crews at six stations have received special training to enable them to go out to a burning vessel and undertake an assessment, getting alongside as safely and quickly as possible so the fire can be extinguished. A special training rig, built to simulate the decks of a ship, has been constructed; a Marine and Tunnel unit is based at Kirkdale carrying special equipment.

A pioneering water-jet powered Rescue Boat was commissioned in 2008, named in honour of the Service's first Chief 'Frank Taylor'; with its associated slide raft it has a capacity of 50 people and is on call for Liverpool Airport as well as general rescue duties on the River Mersey.

*Top left: One of the brigade's pioneering fire-fighting motorbikes. Above: MAN 4-wheel drive pump based at Bootle -Netherton. Below: Marine Rescue jetboat 'Frank Taylor'.*

Road Traffic Collisions, its specially-built Rescue Pump providing advanced capabilities.

All of these services are now provided by just over 800 fire-fighters and 300 other staff, down from a workforce of some 2,000 in 1974 with the number of calls cut from over 60,000 at their peak to under 27,000 in 2010.

An innovative 42-week training course was introduced in 2010 to provide new recruits with a fuller introduction to all aspects of the Service before they become part of an operational crew.

After opening new stations in Liverpool City Centre and at Kensington and a new Engineering Centre, the largest building programme for new fire stations ever seen on Merseyside began in early 2011. Seven more new stations were scheduled to be completed under a PFI contract over the next three years. A revolution in shift patterns and in the provision of cover has

Awarded Beacon status by the Government on no less than three occasions, and having undergone a revolution in almost every aspect of its operations, today's Merseyside Fire and Rescue Service is the best trained, equipped and motivated it has ever been, and dedicated to making the people of Merseyside safer than ever before.

*Top left:* The new Kensington Community Fire Station. **Left:** *Mercedes Benz Small Fires Unit.* **Below:** *A Scania Vema Combined Pump Platform.*

seen the number of duty subsystems work increase from two to seven so that appropriate cover is available to match the peaks and troughs of calls throughout the day.

Merseyside is one of the leading F&RS for Urban Search and Rescue in the UK and no less than three full teams can be provided. The associated Special Rescue Team, also based at Croxteth, responds to all incidents where people are trapped, including

# Let's Go To Knowsley

The word 'Safari' in East Africa's Swahili language means 'Let's go'. And every year thousands say 'Let's go to Knowsley Safari Park'. Knowsley Safari Park, which celebrated its 40th anniversary in 2011, was opened to the public in July, 1971, by the 18th Earl of Derby.

Knowsley Hall dates back to the 12th century and has been in the ownership of the Stanley family since 1385. Lord Stanley was created an Earl by Henry VII on the battlefield of Bosworth. The fourteenth Earl was Prime Minister three times in the 19th century. It was, however, the thirteenth Earl who began Knowsley's association with animals. The famous artist and nonsense-poet Edward Lear was employed there in the 19th century to paint pictures of the thirteenth Earl's collection of 94 species including kangaroos, yak, wildebeest, antelope, eland, gazelle, zebra and the now-extinct quagga from southern Africa. The Earl also kept many species of birds, and in 1848 achieved the first ever captive breeding of budgerigars.

Sadly, this first Knowsley Safari Park came to an end in 1851 with the death of the founder of the menagerie.

Four decades ago the 'safari park' concept of having visitors in cages (their cars) and the animals roaming free, based on the drive-through game reserves of East Africa, was unique.

The estate being only eight miles from Liverpool city centre, Knowsley would become the first safari park to be built so close to a large city and surrounded by suburban housing estates. In spite of some understandable apprehension about large animals (including lions) roaming about, the then County and District councils approved the proposals.

The 18th Earl of Derby obtained planning permission in October 1970 for a game reserve on 346 acres of the estate.

The following year, a month early, in June 1971, ITV screened a Knowsley Safari Park advert by mistake. It created chaos as thousands of people were turned away at the gates.

In July 1971, the Safari Park opened its gates for the first time. One of the key attractions - a herd of 20 elephants – had only just arrived in time having been delayed by a dock strike in Uganda.

Some 200,000 people visited the park in the first month it was open, creating five-mile tailbacks on the surrounding roads. On one day alone 6,500 cars carrying more than 30,000 people passed through the park. And over 150 vehicles broke down!

*Top left:* Founder, the 18th Earl of Derby. *Left:* Tailbacks and car trouble (but still smiling) due to the popularity of park in 1971. *Above:* Then Chief Warden, now General Manager David Ross, with one of the first herd of elephants, pictured in October 1971.

The following year a dolphinarium became the latest addition to the range of attractions. Four dolphins - Duchess, Flipper, Dozy and Scouse – gave daily performances.

In the first two years of opening, the route through Knowsley Safari Park consisted of a 3.5 mile (5.6 km) drive, and the main attractions were lions, cheetahs, monkeys, giraffes, zebra, elephants and various antelopes. The park proved immensely

popular, so in 1973 an extension, including a further 1.5 miles (2.4km) of road, was built. This allowed more animals to be added to the collection on display along the now 5-mile- (8 km) long route, the longest in Britain, including herds of camels, buffalo and white rhino as well as a group of tigers.

Twelve months later, the park introduced its first miniature train ride which is always hugely popular with young visitors. It was replaced by a new train in 1991.

For several years in the 1980s, stages of the RAC Rally were held at Knowsley Safari Park in order to generate extra interest and income for the attraction during off-peak periods.

Meanwhile, in 1982, the park opened a new theatre to stage its daily sea lion shows, one of the highlights of a visit to Knowsley Safari Park for many visitors.

Following the closure of Windsor Safari Park in 1993 Knowsley took delivery of many new animals. These included seven elephants, creating the largest herd in Europe at that time.

The 19th Earl of Derby took over the running of the Knowsley Estate and Safari Park in 1994 and immediately announced a major redevelopment programme. That same year the park was voted the area's top attraction in the prestigious Merseyside Tourism Awards.

*Top left:* A crowded dolphinarium in August 1974. **Bottom left:** A picture that captures perfectly what a uniquely amazing experience a trip to Knowsley Safari Park has been for generations over the last 40 years. **Top right:** Knowsley's miniature train, a hugely popular introduction to the Park. **Above:** The 19th Earl of Derby and family. **Below:** General Manager, David Ross, reveals some of the refurbishments in February 1995.

The safari village was given an exciting new look in 1995 following a major makeover of the restaurant and retail facilities.

Not every story featured good news, however: in 1997 one of the most famous events in the park's history occurred when an unfortunate camel was killed by lightning during a summer thunderstorm.

Meanwhile, the profile of the park soared when it was the subject of a Granada reality TV series in 1998. The attraction soon experienced one of its busiest-ever bank holidays.

The park opened a spectacular new entrance complex, which included additional ticket booths and a new administration office, in 2000. The millennium was also marked by the park's first royal visitor - the Duke of Edinburgh toured the attraction to see the results of a recent £1.2 million programme of improvements.

Good news, however, was followed by bad. In 2001 Britain was hit by a major outbreak of foot-and-mouth disease, the first since 1967. As a result, Knowsley Safari Park was forced to close its gates for many weeks.

Happily, the park soon bounced back; in 2002 a car and coach-friendly route around the monkey jungle was introduced for visitors wishing to avoid its infamous baboons.

Two years later the Safari School welcomed its first children. This purpose-built education centre offers a range of sessions on animal-related themes linked to the National Curriculum.

Knowsley celebrated the arrival of the first-ever critically endangered Pere David's Deer twin fawns to be born in captivity in 2005. And visitor numbers at the Safari Park hit a 30-year high. The attraction welcomed 500,000 people during the year, the highest figure since the early 1970s.

With increasing visitor numbers Knowsley unveiled its new baboon house, built by contractors who had to be fenced in to protect them from the inhabitants of the monkey jungle!

The Aerial Extreme adventure ropes course opened at the park in 2007, featuring 60 obstacles including a 50-foot, parachute-style high-speed drop.

Knowsley's new £600,000 sea lion facility, including a larger pool, rocks, beaches, waterfall effects and an underwater viewing area, opened in 2008.

*Top pictures:* A selection of wonderful animals to be seen in the park. *Centre:* Knowsley's Aerial Extreme adventure. *Left:* The mischievous baboons show that no rooftop luggage box is safe. *Above:* Knowsley Safari Park's Education Department which offers a wide variety of National Curriculum-based sessions.

Meanwhile, those pesky baboons were causing new mischief. In 2009 the park was forced to issue a warning to visitors with rooftop luggage boxes on their cars after the Knowsley baboons mastered the art of breaking into them.

Knowsley Safari Park was voted Britain's top wildlife attraction by viewers of the leading documentary TV channel Eden in 2010.

And things soon got even better: in 2011 no fewer than three white rhino calves (facing page top, second right) Troy, Rosie and Bugo, were born at Knowsley in the space of two months reinforcing the park's conservation credentials and its reputation as a European hotspot for breeding this rare species.

Down the years a few modifications to the original design have had to be made for safety and display reasons. The tigers and lions are now displayed in enclosures within the game reserves, and the elephants have their own paddock in the walk-around section at the end of the safari drive.

Elsewhere, Knowsley's Bug House offers everything from snakes and lizards to spiders and cockroaches, creatures a

world away from the goats, lambs, cattle and horses for the children to enjoy at Lake Farm. Knowsley is also home to an amusement park with a wide selection of rides for all the family.

Quite rightly, Knowsley Safari Park has become one of Merseyside's premier leisure attractions, winning many awards and praise not only for tourism but also for research and conservation work, its education programme, and its support for local indigenous wildlife.

Safari Park General Manager, David Ross, says: "Because of all our new animals and developments over the years there's a huge amount to see and do at the park, which is why we're one of the North West's few genuine all-day attractions. As a result, we offer excellent value for money which is why I am confident that we will continue to attract large numbers of visitors, old and new".

So, 'Safari' - Let's go, to Knowsley!

*Above left:* The Safari Park has a proven track record of breeding exotic animals, some of which are pictured. *Below left:* The park's underwater viewing area, opened in 2008. *Top right:* A visitor favourite - the sea lions show. *Below:* A selection of the species of invertebrate, amphibian and reptile, to be seen in the Bug House.

# Herbert Of Liverpool

Liverpool has far more than its fair share of unforgettable characters. Today, one of its favourite sons is the man most widely known simply as 'Herbert of Liverpool'.

Herbert Howe has been in the hairdressing business for over half a century and based in Liverpool for all of that time. Born in Stoneycroft, the legendary 'Herbert of Liverpool' title is both tongue in cheek swagger and also an association with the city of his birth that Herbert takes very seriously. Almost single-handedly he represents all the prime Liverpudlian characteristics of wit, humour, sharp intelligence and loyalty to his roots. Made famous to a national audience with the television series 'Shampoo' in 1998, Herbert was already one of Liverpool's best-loved citizens before TV stardom beckoned.

Herbert of Liverpool has been serving the people of Liverpool since opening his first salon with £100 at the age of 17; through his career, winning many awards, he has become one of the most respected and famous hairdressers in Britain.

Combining hard work with his larger than life personality and consummate professional skills earned Herbert his first million by the age of 25. It is not by chance that his own particular shade of pink is branded to his own store - neither is it pure chance that a building to his own specification was created for him in the centre of Liverpool. What Herbert takes he always gives back: down the decades he has become well-known for his Mothers Day free hairstyling offer and the huge amount of work he does for various local charities as well as helping more than 500 of his employees to launch their own enterprises.

Herbert appeared in a stage play at the Royal Court "Stairway to Heaven" which ran for 3 weeks

Theatre life was offered to him after his series on Granada Television, 'That Friday Feeling', in 1998. Since then the floodgates opened. Having played the Emperor in Aladdin in 1998 with Julie Goodyear and the Ugly Sister in Cinderella with Stan Boardman, both at the Royal Court Theatre in Liverpool, he then went on to make many TV appearances on ITV, BBC1, BBC2, Channels 4 and 5, and on Satellite TV.

Herbert was very honoured to be offered his very own docu-soap for ITV, Shampoo, which was televised worldwide. Since then he has played Queenie the Cook with Mickey Starke in Dick Whittington at the Royal Court Theatre, Liverpool. He was also delighted to headline in Jack and The Beanstalk as Simple Simon at the Royal Theatre in St. Helens and appear twice in Celebrity Hairdressers Weakest Link with Ann Robinson. He was also asked by Ann to appear on her 1,000th show televised in December 2006.

The business Herbert Howe founded so long ago, 'Herbert of Liverpool', has given the people of

*Top:* Founder, Herbert Howe. **Left:** Herbert aged seventeen pictured with his sister Christine. **Below:** Opening Herbert of Liverpool's 1st Beauty Salon in Church Street with the only Rolls Royce service in Great Britain.

Being fully committed to his hairdressing career he was also able to create one of Britain's most successful training schools, with over 200 students at his flagship premises in his fabulous new premises, the Bling Bling Building, which Herbert opened in July 2006.

Herbert opened his first business in West Derby Road and more than 50 years on he has employed over 5,000 staff, still employing more than sixty today. His

Merseyside luxurious salons offering the most advanced hair and beauty service in the country. Acclaimed by Cosmopolitan Magazine as one of the top eight salons in Great Britain for the Millennium ,the award-winning stylists and a young fashion team with a flair for colour and advanced cutting designs have kept the firm in the forefront of the hairdressing industry.

Herbert of Liverpool now offers a full range of beauty services including Non- Surgical face lifts. It also offers nail-art - young technicians will design and create the most wonderful nails including acrylic and glass nail extensions.

For the more adventurous a Harley Street cosmetic surgeon can offer Botox, the revolutionary injection to take away frown lines, and Restylane for the removal of unwanted facial lines. Also on offer is the Obagi 'Blue Peel' for improvement of skin texture and blemishes as well as removing sun damage and wrinkles to face, hands, neck and chest.

He was delighted to be part of the hair extensions phenomina in it's early days with Diane Marshall of Beverley Hills who personally created extensions for Kate Winslett in Titanic, Gwyneth Paltrow in Shakespeare in Love and many more film and television celebrities. The people of Liverpool can be among the stars by letting Herbert of Liverpool create their very own European-hair non-glue extension.

Hairdressing is only part of Herbert's great enterprise, having ventured into other very successful businesses which include: Beauty Salons, Sun Centres, Ladies and Gents Boutiques, Restaurants and his popular night club Hollywood.

businesses have included nine Hair Salons, six Beauty Salons, three Gents Clothes Boutiques, a Manufacturing Company, a Ladies High Couture Salon and that luxurious city centre night club Hollywood, catering for the youth of Liverpool.

More than twenty years ago, with The Manpower Services Commission, Herbert started one of the first Hairdressing Training Organisations on Merseyside, which led on to North West Training, delivering

*Top left:* Herbert's hairdressers and beauty salon in Paradise Street, 1999. *Above:* Herbert and staff pictured together for the first time. *Below:* Herbert pictured at Liverpool's Pier Head.

Customer Service, Business Admin, I.T., and Retail. As a result several thousand young people have obtained National Vocational Qualifications. Herbert is still involved in training today at his iconic Bling Bling building, at 69 Hanover Street.

Half a century of exemplary commitment to hairdressing has been widely and publicly recognised. Herbert was awarded a lifetime achievement for his services to the hairdressing industry by the Incorporated Guild of Wigmakers, Hairdressers and Perfumers. Herbert was Master of the Guild in 1972-1973 making him the youngest Grand Master since 1860.

He was also asked to be Grand Master in 1977-1979 and was invited to attend the Queen's Garden party at Buckingham Palace.

Herbert was awarded Fellow with Honours in 1987 from the Fellowship for British Hairdressing, of which he had been a member for over twenty five years. He has also

been a member of The National Hairdressing Federation since 1965 and represented Great Britain in New York. In 2008 he also received his lifetime achievement award from The Fellowship for British Hairdressing

Charity has benefited greatly from Herbert's rise. He has had a charitable nature since he started in the hairdressing industry, and has raised nearly £3 million for charity.

His first show for charity was in 1969 in the Philharmonic Hall, Liverpool, for St John Ambulance. He has served on six Lord Mayors Charity Committees and was the instigator of the Live Aid Charity Show on Merseyside.

Herbert also served for three years on The League of Friends, Alder Hey, Liverpool, and served for two years on the committee of the Liverpool Echo's Sunshine Appeal. He was presented to Princess Margaret at the Town Hall for his contribution to the NSPCC. He is a

**Top left:** *Herbert and staff in 1995.* **Left:** *Herbert and comedian Freddie Star share a joke at Herbert of Liverpool's Mothers Day event.* **Above:** *Herbert pictured with mum Queenie Howe and Derek Pace.* **Below:** *At work in the Herbert of Liverpool Training Centre. All teaching staff at the Training Centre are fully qualified within the hairdressing profession and have relevant Teacher/Assesor Qualifications.*

supporter of Children in Need and sends two people to Lourdes by private ambulance every year. He also sponsors the Lord Mayor's Christmas Party for under-privileged children and is the founder of Queenie's Christmas Charity which provides Lunch on Christmas Day for up to five hundred people who would normally be on their own. Named in honour of his late mother and her

love for children, and the magic of Christmas, the Charity was formed to support local people who are less fortunate during the Christmas holidays. His special wish is to reach out and spread a little cheer and happiness to those in need and has an ambition to take Queenie's Christmas nationwide.

Two of Herbert's pet charities are Marie Curie, for which he was delighted to be asked to plant the first of a million daffodils in the Field of Hope, and Macmillan Nurses. He supports every local charity and never refuses to help.

Herbert Howe has devoted his life to helping others achieve their true potential and loves being in the position to help as many people as he can in whatever circumstances they fall into.

Down the years Herbert was offered many opportunities throughout the world, and especially in London, but he has always said the people of Liverpool put him where he is and would never desert them. His love for the city, however, is something that cannot be measured - he even calls himself Herbert of Liverpool.

But if Herbert could be 17 once more might things be different? Herbert Howe is happy to answer that question: "It's been such a wonderful journey. I would do it all again!" The true answer to Herbert's success he says is the wonderful support and values from his family.

*Top: Having fun at a recent Queenie's Christmas charity event. In the top right image Herbert is pictured with two of the charitiy's patrons: Claire Sweeney and Ricky Tomlinson.* **Above left:** *A view inside the Herbert of Liverpool Training Centre.* **Below left and below:** *Herbert inside his iconic Bling Bling building, pictured below.*

# Alfred Price & Sons - The Fruit of Much Labour

It was in 1919 that Alfred Price and his eldest son, Harold, began their potato merchants business at Burscough Bridge, Lancashire. The company has been importing fresh fruit and vegetables from around the world since the 1930s. Today, procurement teams are personally involved in selecting produce from specialised growers in major producing countries across the globe.

Five more of Alfred's sons joined the family firm in the 1920s and 1930s, opening a number of depots in Yorkshire supplying potatoes to wholesale and retail customers throughout the country.

In 1927, Harold started travelling by train to Europe, particularly to Spain and France, arranging supplies, principally of potatoes and onions from Spain, much of which were imported through the Port of Liverpool.

In those times the traders in Victoria Street were supplying almost half of the fruit and vegetables imported into the United Kingdom. This was an important hub of the fruit trade, with buyers travelling from wholesale markets throughout the country to the fruit auctions which took place there.

Liverpool's Fruit Exchange, No.10-16 Victoria Street, was built in the 1880s as a railway goods depot for the London & North Western Railway and was converted into a fruit exchange in 1923 by James B Hutchins. The building was originally

*Top: An early 20th century view of Queen's Square fruit and veg market. **Left:** Founder, Alfred Price. **Below:** A fruit auction at Victoria Street, circa 1920s/30s.*

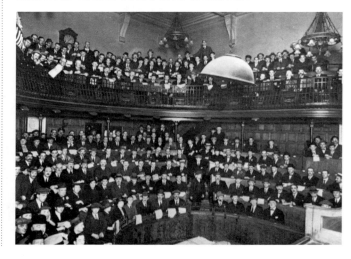

constructed to serve Exchange Station on Tithebarn Street (the first station was built in 1850 and a larger version constructed in 1886-8; this eventually closed in 1950). After its change of use in 1923 the Fruit Exchange became the main trading point for fruit produce within the city and dealt with the majority of fruit imports coming into Liverpool. Warehouses in the Mathew Street area were used to store the fruit sold at the exchange. In the late 20th century the lower ground floor would be converted into separate public houses.

Within the Fruit Exchange, with its unique interior where two auctions could take place simultaneously, the bigger players did their deals. Harold Price, however, realised that the only way of selling his imports was to stand on the steps of the Fruit Exchange to catch buyers as they were leaving the auctions. This type of trading was discouraged by the commissionaires who were employed by the auction brokers to make sure that trading did not take place on the steps.

There would be some difficult times ahead, however, when plans for expansion were halted as a civil war had broken out in Spain in 1936 and would last for three years: those hostilities would seriously disrupt supplies from that country. The war ended in April 1939 and brought with it the assumption that problem-free trade would resume, only to be dashed a few months later when Hitler invaded Poland and Britain and France declared war on Germany.

The next six years would not only see the end of imports from occupied France but also the serious disruption of food imports of every kind. Hitler aimed to starve Britain and launched his wolf packs of U-boats charged with the task of sinking every ship headed for Britain. And even if the ships arrived safely they would find dock facilities bombed by the Luftwaffe.

Happily, the firm was able to continue trading. After the Second World War a number of importers opened fruit sales rooms in Victoria Street and Alfred Price & Sons Ltd acquired accommodation in one of those rooms.

During the 1950s and 1960s Harold Price again travelled the world, making contacts in South Africa, Australia, New Zealand

*Above:* Staff at Bursgough Bridge pictured in the late 1940s.
*Below:* Temple fruit sales room in Victoria Street in the early 1950s.

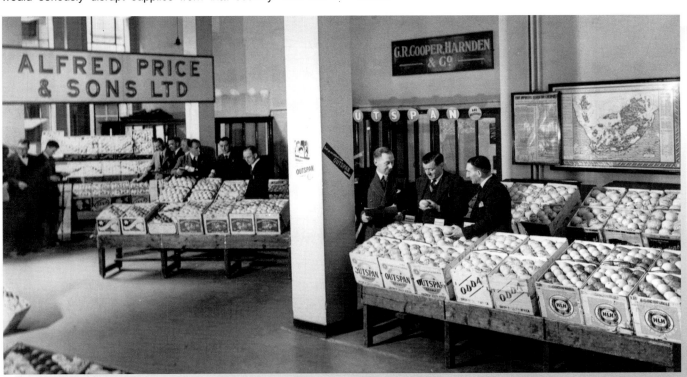

and South America, and developing the company into one of the UK's major fruit and vegetable importers.

From the Gladstone Dock to Toxteth, many of the berths were handling fruit and vegetable cargos. During these years Alfred Price & Sons Ltd employed a team of dockmen whose job was to arrange the loading of their vehicles.

There was a weekly arrival from the Canary Islands of tomatoes, with the fruit being sold from the docks. Alfred Price & Sons Ltd employed salesmen who worked at the tomato berths.

Harold Price's son, Tony, joined the business in 1960 and continued developing contacts with the best overseas growers to make sure that Alfred Price & Sons Ltd was able to offer the best quality fruit to customers. Many of those growers are still supplying the company today. Tony Price became Managing Director in the mid 1970s at a time of a changing pattern of trade from Europe, with more and more fruit being transported by road and rail, and the importance of the Port of Liverpool was declining. A consequence of these changes was that in 1980 Alfred Price & Sons Ltd moved to a new purpose-built office and

warehouse site in Kings Dock Street where the company continued to operate for the next twenty years.

During those years, with the emerging power of the major supermarkets, the trade changed direction away from the retail and wholesale business. The amalgamation, in 1995, with Trifruit Ltd, a company specialising in the importation of fruit for supermarkets, helped Alfred Price & Sons Ltd diversify, to become an important supplier to some of the major supermarkets.

The family connection continued into the fourth generation when Tony Price's son, Simon Price, joined the company in the 1990s: he is today's Managing Director.

The business moved again in 1999 to its purpose-built site in Knowsley Business Park, in Prescot. This building was designed for the supermarket trade, with temperature-controlled facilities and a packing area for pre-packed fruit and vegetables.

Alfred Price & Sons Ltd now employs more than forty full-time staff, many of whom have been with the company for many years. The Alfred Price team, which has a strong supply base and excellent sourcing, works closely with an established worldwide family of growers, stretching as far as Chile,

*Top left: Father and son, Harold and Tony Price. **Bottom:** The company's Kings Dock Street premises pictured in 1980 after their move from Victoria Street. **Above:** All products imported by the company are subject to rigorous quality control by their highly professional technical department.*

South Africa and New Zealand in the Southern Hemisphere as well as incorporating European producing countries, in order to provide 12 months continuity to customers.

Seedless Grapes represent an important part of the product portfolio and the dedication of specialised grape growers throughout the world ensures that Alfred Price maintains its reputation as one of the UK's leading suppliers of the complete range of this popular product.

Alfred Price's customer portfolio covers every section within the fresh produce industry, including all categories within the multiple sector, as well as the wholesale trade and the catering industry. The company is proud to have an experienced sales team which focus on meeting the demands of customers' every day.

Despite the changes down the decades the company maintain its traditional role as a major supplier to the wholesale market ,which remains a key section of the business.

Alongside this, however, Alfred Price is a growing provider to multiples who have their own special requirements: the company has the resources to meet them, not least the ability to supply all year round and to label and package produce in line with individual customer's requirements. The company is always looking for new sources of supply in order to keep multiple customers at the forefront of their business. The procurement team is constantly working on new product development, travelling around the world to source products through a large network of international contacts.

Meanwhile, Alfred Price is keen to continue to develop its IT systems and is proud to have recently installed an electronic Stock Management system in its warehouse and fridges to ensure stock is located and used in the most productive way,

always keeping produce as fresh as possible and in the optimum conditions. Separate storage facilities are used for products that are not temperature compatible.

The company's facility boasts a generous warehouse site which includes a 36,000 square foot cold store chamber with the capacity for a total of 1,500 pallets. There are seven loading bays to ensure minimum turnaround times, allowing the company to maintain complete field to door cool-chain continuity. The site also incorporates a purpose built pack house and label office so that Alfred Price can offer its customers a comprehensive packing, sorting and labelling service.

Today, the company is one of the major importers into the United Kingdom. Alfred Price would have been proud to see what has been achieved by the firm he founded almost a century ago.

***Top and below:*** *Interior and exterior views of Alfred Price & Son Ltd's purpose-built site in Knowsley Business Park, Prescot.* ***Above:*** *Managing Director Simon Price and father Tony, 2011.*

# LBK Packaging – The Complete Package

LBK – Levy Brothers & Knowles Ltd – was established in Liverpool in 1831 by two brothers Eustace and Benjamin Levy. They were soon joined by George Knowles. Sadly, George Knowles was killed in an accident at an early age, but the Levys, followed by their sons, continued to be involved in the business until the early 1940s.

The partnership had begun after spotting the potential of the hessian sack business in the booming trade that was starting to develop in Liverpool.

In those days and indeed right up until after the Second World War most goods and produce were packed and transported in hessian sacks and Liverpool would be at the very centre of this multi-million pound world trade in sacking material.

Jute, from which hessian is made, was imported from the Indian sub-continent where ten million bales a year were once

produced. Dundee was the British centre of hessian manufacture until Indian production began in the 1870s. Hessian was transported from the Liverpool docks to factories by a convoy of horses and carts where a workforce of several hundred was waiting to turn the cloth into various types of bags.

LBK expanded rapidly. Offices and factories were subsequently established in Dundee, Bristol, Glasgow, Hull, Belfast and London. The Glasgow office is still open today.

Growth continued during the 19th and early 20th centuries – though sadly during the First World War many employees who were called up would never return.

By the time of the Second World War the company had several factories around Liverpool and was responsible for producing

**Above:** *A Levy Brothers & Knowles Ltd advert from 1926.*
**Below:** *LBK's Park Lane premises in the 1970s.*

Minister William Ewart Gladstone and also having been the home of one of Liverpool's first breweries. Following the acquisition the front of the building was completely cleaned up and restored to its former glory and today it is one of the most impressive buildings in Duke Street.

In 2002, following the redevelopment of the city centre, the company relocated to a new 30,000 sq ft factory in Knowsley Business Park from where it continues to operate along with its offices in Glasgow.

Today, the company supplies a complete range of industrial packaging from paper, polythene and FIBCs (Flexible Intermediate Bulk Container or 'big bags') to cardboard products, as well as small amounts of hessian. In addition the experienced and loyal workforce is continually looking at designing new types of packaging and has recently developed and brought to the market a new type of cardboard A frame which is wholly recyclable and capable of transporting glass and other products in excess of a half a tonne in weight.

The company's products are sold all over the UK, Europe the USA and China.

LBK has had a long and fascinating history. From its current bases in Knowsley and Glasgow and with its extensive range of products the future looks equally exciting. Having begun life in the 19th century the name of Levy Brothers and Knowles looks set fair into continue to the 22nd century.

millions of sandbags to aid the war effort. Unfortunately, being located near to the docks the buildings were subject to regular bombing raids and the main offices in Brunswick Street along with factories in Batchelor Street and Henry Street were completely destroyed. However, despite the best efforts of the Luftwaffe the company managed to keep trading throughout the war years and continued to produce sandbags along with other types of hessian sacks.

After the war the company operated from its premises on Park Lane. The factory in Henry Street was then completely rebuilt during the 1950s.

Packaging trends now began to change with the introduction of paper and polythene.

Eric McLennan Snr had joined the company at the age of 14 as an office junior in the Glasgow office. He worked his way up to become Managing Director and remained with the company until his retirement in 1985. In 1980 he was succeeded as Managing Director by his son Eric McLennan Jnr who started with the company in 1972 and since then has overseen the expansion and diversification of the business.

During the 1980s and 1990s the company made several acquisitions in order to widen its range of products. These included the Liverpool branch of William Noble & Son, Selman Sacks, Tyrrell Plastics, Presentation Packaging, Derwen Polythene and Brown Brough Liverpool.

With the purchase of Brown Brough the company also acquired the building it occupied at 64-66 Duke Street. The building had a colourful history having once been owned by Victorian Prime

*Top left:* The entrance to 64 Duke Street, former premises of LBK. *Centre:* Examples of products manufactured by LBK: Looplifter bags (left) paper reels (top) and a pharmaceutical box. *Below:* The company's 30,000 sq ft factory in Knowsley Business Park.

# Wrenco Construction

**W**renco. Does the name ring a bell? It should do, for the firm has been involved in innumerable civil engineering projects around Liverpool since 1964.

The founders of Wrenco (Contractors) Ltd - Terry Bolland, Jimmy McMahon, Tom McGuire and Emlyn 'Em' Roberts - first met through a common involvement with a self-build housing group. In such schemes the members, whether tradesmen, professionals or labourers, teamed up on an equal basis to provide a home for each member through their collective toil.

The notion occurred to Terry and Jimmy that the same ethos might be successfully applied to a business venture and they in turn put their idea to Tom and Emlyn who readily joined up. Thus the 'gang of four' pooled the talents of two foremen, an accountant/business adviser and a quantity surveyor. All they were short of was work.

The very first job was a Labour-Only Contract to excavate by hand the foundations of an office development at Widnes. Some of the stanchion bases were more than twenty feet deep but Jimmy and Tom tore into it with such verve and vigour that it convinced the site agent that he need look no further for resources for the remainder of the contract - nor did the agent baulk when Emlyn arrived each Friday to 'agree the measure' and ensure that every inch of work and every drop of sweat was paid for at premium rates. Extra labour was recruited and the contract went on for some six months, at the end of which there was a very handy lump of working capital in the bank.

To protect the fragile finances of the fledgling firm an arrangement was struck that although the on-site people would work full-time for a basic salary the two professional types would keep their existing occupations and take only a fraction of the same salary, integrating only as the firm grew. It would be 1968 before all four were fully committed on an equal basis, each one both learning from and working for the others.

Meanwhile, the momentum was maintained with cable-laying contracts from the G.P.O. and domestic garage building for the surrounding local authorities. As the Sixties drew to a close the company had earned sufficient respect from local authorities to be awarded major road contracts such as duelling of the A41 New Chester Road at Bebington and also of Borough Road, Birkenhead, followed by the re-vamping of the Mersey Tunnel approaches at Birkenhead. There were also two major sewerage schemes at Hoylake and Banks which were won and duly completed within budget and on time.

*Above right:* Ben Peters who in 1970 at the age of 65 joined the firm as clerical assistant. *Below left:* The 1982 Garden Festival site. *Below:* Lifting out the 100 year old pedestrian bridge on the Leeds-Liverpool canal. The original bridge was the widest on the canal, designed as a major thoroughfare for the thousands of dockers from their homes on the terraced streets of Liverpool, down to work at the docks.

Another scheme at Ormskirk provided special interest for Wrenco. The council received letters from the local residents praising both the courtesy of the men, and the progress of their work. In recognition of this the Chairman, in his official car, decided to make a surprise visit to the site to drink a Champagne toast to Jimmy McMahon and his drainage team! It was fortunate for Wrenco that the story, with pictures, was picked up by the national daily papers which provided welcome publicity.

By now people had been recruited, who, with the founders, would become the bedrock of the company: Don Lucas, Chief Q.S. and Contracts Manager, who would lead the operations in the 1980s and 90s; Rick Hudson (Engineer), John Coady, Tommy Brennan, Ted Wickham, Martin McGuire and the late Mick Flanagan (all Foremen) and good old Ben Peters, clerical assistant extraordinaire who in 1970, at the age of 65, asked if he could join the company for one day as a trial and never missed a single day, six days a week, until he passed away in 1987. Also at that time the company acquired a site and built its present premises on the industrial estate at Sefton Lane, Maghull.

The 1970s brought work from the Development Corporations at Runcorn, Warrington, Skelmersdale and Central Lancs. The company began recruiting local school leavers, two of whom, Dave Brooks and Mike Williams, would eventually hold key positions in Wrenco.

The Merseyside Development Corporation, set up in the 1980s to change the face of Liverpool, provided many contracts for Wrenco during its fourteen year regeneration process from the initial Garden Festival Project through to the construction of the Leeds St/Old Hall St/Gt Howard St junction in 1996. The 1990s brought a rash of town centre refurbishments in Liverpool, Kirby, Manchester, Leigh, Tyldsley and Widnes for Wrenco whilst in 2000 the company completed the £3 million refurbishment of the Princes Dock Basin at the Pier Head.

The first decade of the new millennium saw the Company complete £15million of work on schools and hospitals across Liverpool and the wider region, as well as its largest ever single job, a £5million contract for work at the new underground gas storage facility in Northwich, Cheshire – completed within 10

months by the team of Tommy McMahon and Paul Richardson. After a management buy-out in 2002, the new decade also saw the introduction of new faces, such as Tony Carney, who would go on to establish new client relationships and hold directorships at the Company.

Though remaining a medium sized firm, Wrenco is one with strong capabilities – and it remains just as ready for a challenge now as it was on the day it was conceived by those four idealistic young men back in 1964.

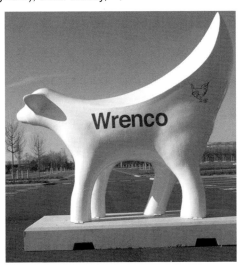

*Top left:* Refurbishment of the Princes Dock. ***Above:*** *Still going strong, with a combined total of one hundred and twenty-seven years service at Wrenco; (left to right) Bert Savage (twenty-five years), John Coady (forty-four years), Wally Burns (thirty-five years) and Ted Wickham (thirty-three years).* ***Left:*** *The Wrencolambanana, part of the Liverpool 2008 Capital of Culture year.*

# Silverbeck Rymer - Putting Customers First

**S**ilverbeck Rymer Solicitors have come a long way from humble beginnings. From one man's vision in small premises above a jaunty local pub on Dale Street, to one of the UK's leading law firms, the account of Silverbeck Rymer's success is interesting and varied. One fact has remained constant, however, - their passion for always putting the customer first.

The firm's history began with a young Solicitor called Nathan Silverbeck, establishing a small firm in 1946. Nathan established himself in premises above Rigby's pub in Dale Street as a general law firm with a strong bias towards domestic conveyancing. The firm soon began to flourish and in 1949 Sidney Brayde joined the business as a Partner.

Further expansion led to Jim Rymer joining as an article clerk in 1979, he later became a Partner and to this day remains at the helm as Chairman. Jim was subsequently joined by his brother Charles as a trainee solicitor who today is SR's Compliance Partner.

In the 1980s the firm began its period of rapid growth and in 1993 moved into Heywood's building located within the heart of the business district within the city centre. Previously a bank, Silverbeck Rymer had to make functional use of the vault which remained in the basement, which they did by creating a legal library for the use of all staff!

As the expansion continued, Silverbeck Rymer opened up a second office in Chelmsford in 1997 and an office in Manchester in 2002.

As the business grew in size, so did the level of expertise and

*Top left:* Senior Partner Jim Rymer. **Above:** Sidney Brayde. **Below:** A view of Dale Street at the time Nathan Silverbeck established the firm.

Manchester operation into the new waterfront building at a time when changes were taking place across the city with the Capital of Culture preparations.

Over the last few years, the growth of the business has been driven by claimant work and in 2007 a strategic decision was made to focus on this area and SR became a claimant only firm. This decision opened up new opportunities for growth and within months saw new clients partnering with SR.

The legal industry has seen many changes over the last 60 years which has kept the minds of SR employees challenged, however, with a strong culture for hard work and excellent customer service instilled within the company and its people, SR have always managed to overcome these challenges.

Over the course of the next few years, SR invested heavily in technology and, to this day reinvests a substantial amount back into the business to ensure that they are true to their roots and continue to deliver a first class service through their people and processes.

SR were able to create a dedicated catastrophic unit offering clients who had suffered extensive, life changing Injuries a service which covered rehabilitation, alternative housing, full time liaison and the funds with which to support their recovery.

The nooks and crannies of Heywood's building were no longer able to accommodate SR's growth and the decision was made to move outside of the city centre to a building which could support the ambitious growth plans the firm still had.

Silverbeck Rymer moved to an old warehouse located on the Brunswick dock and converted the drafty old storage building into a modern office environment. Where once there were piles of post and mailbags there are now rows of desks featuring the latest technology in a modern open plan set up. With the larger premises completed SR were able to amalgamate their

From the days of Silverbeck and Brayde, the organisational structure is now spearheaded by a Board of Directors with a wealth of experience within professional services.

Jim and his brother Charles, have remained true to the founding principals set by Nathan Silverbeck and have created their own legacy which they hope will continue in the future on a national and local scale .

*Top left: The firm's former premises in Brunswick Street. Below: The converted warehouse on the Brunswick Dock, home of Silverbeck Rymer since 2005.*

# Nugent Care - Supporting The Community Since 1881

Nugent Care is one of the oldest and largest charities in Liverpool. The organisation offers a wide range of support to vulnerable and disadvantaged adults and children throughout Merseyside and parts of the North West of England.

The scope and breadth of Nugent Care's work is immense as it is constantly evolving to meet the changing needs of society. Providing support to over 7,000 people each year, Nugent Care's services included: Support for people wishing to and who have been adopted - Residential care for adults with dementia, metal health needs and physical disabilities - Support for people with learning disabilities - Respite care for children with disabilities - Schools for young people with special education needs - Homeless and welfare support - Community groups for deaf people and hard of hearing people - Volunteer and befriending schemes.

The origins of Nugent Care date back to the nineteenth century and the pioneering work of Monsignor James Nugent. Father Nugent, as he preferred to be known, although he had been given the title of Monsignor in 1892 by Pope Leo X111, was a Catholic Priest who was born in Hunter Street, Liverpool. He devoted his whole life to serving the people of his home city.

During Father Nugent's early years as a Priest at St Nicolas Church, Copperas Hill, over 300,000 people arrived in Liverpool to escape the potato famine in Ireland. This mass immigration resulted in appalling living conditions for the poor, consequently people died in their thousands of fever, diarrhoea and cholera.

It was common to find orphaned children huddled in doorways and railway arches for shelter due to the increasing number of adult deaths in the city. Father Nugent witnessed this and campaigned for social reform in the city first for children and later on in his

life for adults. In a speech about the number of homeless children on the streets Father Nugent described the terrible conditions: "They roam unheeded about those crowded thoroughfares and along those five miles of docks, desolate and homeless wanderers, without a heart to love them or a hand to guide them. How many die of actual starvation and

are buried in the pauper's heap without a mourner to follow their coffin, or a single tear shed over their grave? Poor children of the streets!"

*Top left: Portrait of Father Nugent (1822-1905), from the Walker Art Gallery, Liverpool. Left: A Sketch of Hunter Street - the birthplace of Father Nugent. Above: An example of the conditions documented by Father Nugent – Cholera cartoon from Punch, 1852. Below and inset: The Clarence Reformatory School Ship for Boys, docked in the River Mersey.*

Nugent Care
**Good Shepherd appeal**

With support from various high standing individuals in the city including the Lord Mayor of the time, and religious orders both Catholic and non Catholic, Father Nugent began setting up a series of hostels and schools, for boys and girls including the Clarence Reformatory Ship for Boys, the Notre Dame School for Girls and St Edward's College.

In 1863 Father Nugent became the Chaplain of Walton Prison. The number of female prisoners there outnumbered the number of men. This encouraged Father Nugent to set up the House of Providence in West Dingle, a home for single mothers and their babies, and St Saviour's Women's Refuge in Paul Street which went onto help over 9000 women.

On 16 April, 1881, Father Nugent and his supporters founded the Liverpool Catholic Children's Protection Society, which after several name changes including; the Catholic Children's Society, Liverpool Catholic Social Services and the Nugent Care Society, became simply known as Nugent Care in 2005.

By the time of Father Nugent's death in 1905, he had given homes, hope and valuable skills to thousands of people. His dedication, courage and pioneering work laid the foundations for the support that Nugent Care offers to this very day.

In 2011 Nugent Care received the honour of the Freedom of the City from Liverpool Council in acknowledgement of the work of the charity's founder and for the vital support the organisation has provided to the most vulnerable and disadvantaged people in Liverpool and the surrounding areas since 1881.

*Top left:* An early sketch of Notre Dame Training College. *Above left and left:* At work in the laundry room of the refuge shelter for women in Paul Street. *Top right (both pictures):* The Good Shepherd appeal started by Bishop Whiteside in the early 1900s which is a crucial part of Nugent Care's fundraising activities and Nugent Care's Charity Shop in Allerton Road, Liverpool. *Above:* Nugent Care White (goods) Christmas Appeal 2010 with Patron, Phil Thompson (former LFC Captain).

# The Millgrain Group - Going With the Grain

The Millgrain Group is a range of businesses that have been operating in Liverpool since the early 1970s. Although the companies are diverse, they all have strong ties to the Port of Liverpool.

Founding company of the Group was Millford Grain, a grain-merchanting business sourcing, pricing and shipping high quality milling wheat from around the world. It occupies a niche role in providing an import service to both smaller independent flour millers and national organisations. By grouping several customers onto one vessel, and running a monthly shipping programme, the company is able to provide all with economies of scale on freight from North America.

Millford Grain was established in Bristol in 1949. It relocated to Liverpool in the early 1970s with the completion of the Royal Seaforth Grain terminal in the Port of Liverpool. This deep water facility allowed the company to use larger 60,000 metric tonne panamax vessels.

Backhouse Bloore Ltd was incorporated into the Group in 1979 and operates primarily as a ship's agency company, providing a logistical support service for international ship-owners coming to Liverpool. Other roles that Backhouse Bloore has undertaken over the years are stevedoring , and also superintending, which offered a quality overview in sampling, testing and supervising of goods arriving in Liverpool.

Mersey Asphalt was incorporated in 1999. A 50:50 joint venture with Tarmac Ltd, an asphalt plant was built on Seaforth Dock to provide asphalt and macadam products to the local building industry and local councils in and around Merseyside.

Michael Groves established the basis for the Group by buying grain merchanting businesses Charlton Backhouse and Millford Grain soon after they had relocated to Liverpool in 1970. Previously he had worked for Millford Grain in Bristol, and prior to that Tradax, the commodity-trading arm of Cargill plc in the City of London. He was joined by business partner Clive Ratcliff in 1980, who had known Michael at Tradax in London. Clive worked for Millford Grain until his retirement in 2009.

**Top left:** Founder, Michael Groves. **Above:** MV Rosetti, the first ship to dock at Royal Seaforth Grain Terminal. **Below:** MV W.D.Cargill, 70,000mt, the largest ship to dock in Seaforth.

Alistair Groves, Michael's son has now taken the role as Managing Director and manages the team at Millgrain on a day-to-day basis. Alistair's brother Henry also worked for the company for 15 years before moving to Canada.

Originally the company was based in the Corn Exchange, in Liverpool city centre. The Group headquarters is now based in an old merchant's house in Waterloo, not far from the Port of Liverpool. At the Seafield House headquarters there are ten employees, and four on-site with Mersey Asphalt.

Millford Grain had to endure the difficulties of the national dock strike of 1972 and Britain's entry into the E.E.C. in 1973, which brought about new, and very high import tariffs, making imported wheat that much more expensive. However, Millford was soon able to benefit from renewed demand for higher quality bread and baked products, needing high quality wheat, as GATT forced the EEC to lower the high import tariffs.

Currently, Millford Grain ships about 200,000mt of high quality Canadian Spring Wheat into Liverpool, and a further 50,000mt to Tilbury in London. Customers include Rank Hovis, ADM, Allied Mills, Whitworth and Carrs, to name but a few.

Since the mid-1990s a major relationship is the one that the company forged with Warburtons. Millford Grain has the responsibility of shipping all of Warburtons Canadian wheat, that is used in their bread making process. The high quality Canadian wheat helps to provide the added quality for which Warburtons bread is renowned.

Mersey Asphalt has managed to maintain its focus throughout the years that it has been operating, through the good times and the leaner years following the credit crunch of 2008, when the construction industry took a significant knock. It continues to follow its business plan and maintains its commitment to supplying quality materials to contractors in the Merseyside area.

Millford Grain continues to provide an invaluable service to flour millers in the UK. The company continues to operate in an increasingly volatile world market, with price and supply of food commodities more unpredictable from year to year. The excellent relationships that have been forged, and the trust that has been built over the years, continue to provide the bedrock for the success of the business.

*Above: Bird's eye view of Seaforth Docks. Below: Mersey Asphalt Limited.*

# ACKNOWLEDGMENTS

The publishers would like to sincerely thank a number of individuals and organisations

for their help and contribution to this publication.

Getty Images - www.gettyimages.co.uk

Press Association - www.pressassociation.com

Colin Wilkinson - www.streetsofliverpool.co.uk

Steve Howe - www.chesterwalls.info/gallery/oldpics

Chris Kelly - www.flickr.com/photos/jackamanfan/